MOVING WITH CHILDREN

A Parent's Guide To Moving With Children

Thomas T. Olkowski, Ph.D.

Lynn Parker, LCSW

GYLANTIC PUBLISHING COMPANY
Littleton, Colorado

Although the authors have done research to ensure the accuracy and completeness of the information contained in this book, the authors and publisher assume no responsibility for errors, inaccuracies, omissions or any other inconsistency herein. Data contained herein are the most complete and accurate available as this book goes to print. Please bear in mind that meanings can vary due to personal interpretation.

To order additional copies:

GYLANTIC PUBLISHING COMPANY
P.O. Box 2792
Littleton, Colorado 80161-2792
1-800-828-0113
Add $2.00 to each order for shipping and handling

Printed in the United States by Gilliland Printing, Inc.
The text is printed with soy ink.

Copyright © 1993 by Thomas T. Olkowski, Ph.D. and
Lynn Parker, LCSW

All rights reserved. No part of this publication may be reproduced or transmitted in any form or by any means, electronic or mechanical, photocopy, recording or any information storage or retrieval system, without permission in writing from the publisher.

Library of Congress Cataloging-in-Publication-Data

Olkowski, Thomas T., 1943-
 Moving with children : a parent's guide to moving with children / Thomas T. Olkowski, Lynn Parker.
   p.   cm.
 Includes bibliographical references and index.
 ISBN 1-880197-08-1 : $12.95
 1. Moving, Household--Psychological aspects. 2. Child psychology. 3. Parent and child. I. Parker, Lynn. II. Title.
TX307.043   1993
648'.9'083--dc20   93-19123
                                                                   CIP

For their love and support, this book is dedicated to:
Jeanne and Colin, Mom and Dad   (T.O.)
Mom, Dad and Walter; Martha, Claire, Jim and Tom   (L.P.)

I am a part of all that I have met;
Yet all experience is an arch wherethrough
Gleams that untravelled world whose margin fades
For ever and for ever when I move.

 Alfred Lord Tennyson
Ulysses

A portion of the proceeds from the sale of this book is being donated by the authors to agencies working with the homeless in the Denver area.

EMMAUS PUBLIC LIBRARY
11 E. MAIN STREET
EMMAUS, PA 18049

Table of Contents

About the Authors ix
Introduction xi

CHAPTER 1

How Do You Pack The Family's Feelings? 3
    Two Families on the Move
    The Preparation Stage
    The Work Stage
    The Settling-in Stage

CHAPTER 2

Why Moving Causes Problems For Kids 17
    Potential Preparation Stage Stressors on Children
    Children's Emotional Responses to Preparation Stage Stressors
    Potential Work Stage Stressors on Children
    Children's Emotional Responses to Work Stage Stressors
    Potential Settling-in Stage Stressors on Children
    Children's Emotional Responses to Settling-in Stage Stressors
    Signs of Move-related Stress in Children

CHAPTER 3

How Kids Feel About Moving 33
    What Kids Have to Say About Moving
    Discussion Tips for Parents
    Kids' Questions About Moving

CHAPTER 4
When You Move Matters (Sometimes) 41
When You Talk About Moving Matters

CHAPTER 5
Practical Moving Tools For Families 49
Premove Supplies for Kids
Some Unheard-of Moving Tips for Parents
A Premove Checklist for Kids
A Premove Checklist for Parents
A Premove Calendar for Families

CHAPTER 6
Helping Kids Say Goodbye 61
Special Goodbyes for Special Moves

CHAPTER 7
Practical Packing For Families 69
Practical Packing Supplies for Kids
A Chaos-Survival Kit for Parents
When Moving Day Finally Arrives

CHAPTER 8
Well, We're Here. Now What? 79
Moving-in Supplies for Kids
Some Unheard-of Unpacking Tips for Parents
A Post-move Checklist for Families
A Post-Move Calendar for Families

CHAPTER 9
Exploring Your New Neighborhood 89
Tools for Exploring Your Neighborhood
The Neighborhood Discovery Board
A Neighborhood Map
The Neighborhood Yellow Pages
Grab Bag Explorers
Let Your Fingers Do the Exploring

CHAPTER 10
Making Friends In A New School
And Neighborhood 105
   Tips From Kids to Kids About Making Friends
   Some Tips for Shy Kids
   Discussion Tips for Parents

CHAPTER 11
Letters To Roger 115

CHAPTER 12
Some Don'ts About Moving And Making Friends 123
   Some Don'ts for Kids
   Some Don'ts for Parents

CHAPTER 13
What Kids Want From Parents 131
   Some Other Things Parents Can Do for Kids

CHAPTER 14
Going To A New School 139
   Some Tips for Teachers

CHAPTER 15
The Million-mile Move:
Moving To A Foreign Country 147
   Getting There is Part of the Job
   Adjusting to a New Culture

CHAPTER 16
Some Final Thoughts About Moving 161

Sources 165

Note On The Moving Survey 166

An Invitation To Parents And Kids 168

Readings For Children 169
    Non-fiction
    Fiction
    Video Cassette
    Audiotapes

Readings For Parents 172

Resource Organizations For Families 174

Acknowledgments 178

Authors' Note 180

Index I–1

About the Authors

Thomas T. Olkowski, Ph.D., a clinical psychologist, and Lynn Parker, LCSW, a social worker, have been in private practice with children, families and adults in Denver, Colorado since 1977.

Prior to beginning private practice, Tom and Lynn worked as mental health consultants for the Cherry Creek School District and the Arapahoe Mental Health Center in Englewood, Colorado, where they developed a preventive mental health program in the schools and together founded and coordinated the Rocky Mountain Conference on Schools and Mental Health from 1974 until 1980.

Tom has taught as an adjunct associate professor of human relations for Webster University in the United States, Iceland and Bermuda and has published articles and poetry on topics related to humor, sports and mental health.

Lynn is presently an instructor and supervisor in the Family Therapy Training Program of Colorado and an adjunct faculty instructor in the Graduate School of Social Work at the University of Denver. She also conducts workshops for women and couples.

Both Tom and Lynn have made television and radio appearances and presented numerous workshops and training seminars for schools, professional organizations and community groups on the topics of parenting, personal growth and interpersonal relationships.

Introduction

"I don't want to move. I've lived here the longest in my whole life, and my friends are here. If we were moving close by, I wouldn't mind so much, but moving 120 miles is hard. And making new friends is going to be hard because I won't know anyone. When my mom was a kid, she had to move. I bet she remembers how it felt." –John P., 6th Grade

These words of a twelve-year-old boy facing an end-of-the-school-year move reflect the sentiments of many of the six million children whose families relocate each year in the United States. For youngsters moving is often a difficult experience that entails some degree of sadness, apprehension and emotional upheaval. As John reminds us, most parents, whether they remember it or not, have endured moves that caused behavioral reactions and emotions similar to those their children now face.

If you think back to your own childhood, the anticipation of a family move, regardless of the reasons or the possible excitement involved, raised the spectre of lonely days in an unfamiliar place surrounded by strangers, longings for abandoned friends whose joyous play continued in your absence, solitary walks down crowded corridors in a strange school where no one seemed to notice your presence and the overwhelming dread that you would never make a new friend or be accepted in a community that you had no say in choosing. Life as you knew it was over, and in your heart you believed, at least for fleeting moments, that you could never be happy again despite anything your parents might say or do.

Now years later as you prepare for your family's present move, you can anticipate that despite your many reassurances, your own youngsters will most likely experience some of the same sadness, fear and dread at the thought of moving that you once did as a child.

Moving With Children is a book designed to help you as a parent understand and deal with the many feelings and behaviors that children express when families move. It is a collection of practical and effective suggestions to allow you to help your entire family deal with the various stages of moving from planning and discussing the move with your children to saying goodbye, packing and unpacking, exploring your new community, meeting new friends, and settling into your new home.

The advice presented here is meant for both children and adults and is based upon the authors' many years of professional family counseling experience as well as ideas obtained from over 2,500 elementary and middle school youngsters who shared their thoughts and feelings with us in response to a specially designed moving survey.

The purpose of this book is to help you and your children create a spirit of mutual support and teamwork that will eliminate some of the heartaches involved in moving and allow all of you to experience the enjoyment and sense of adventure that a family move can offer.

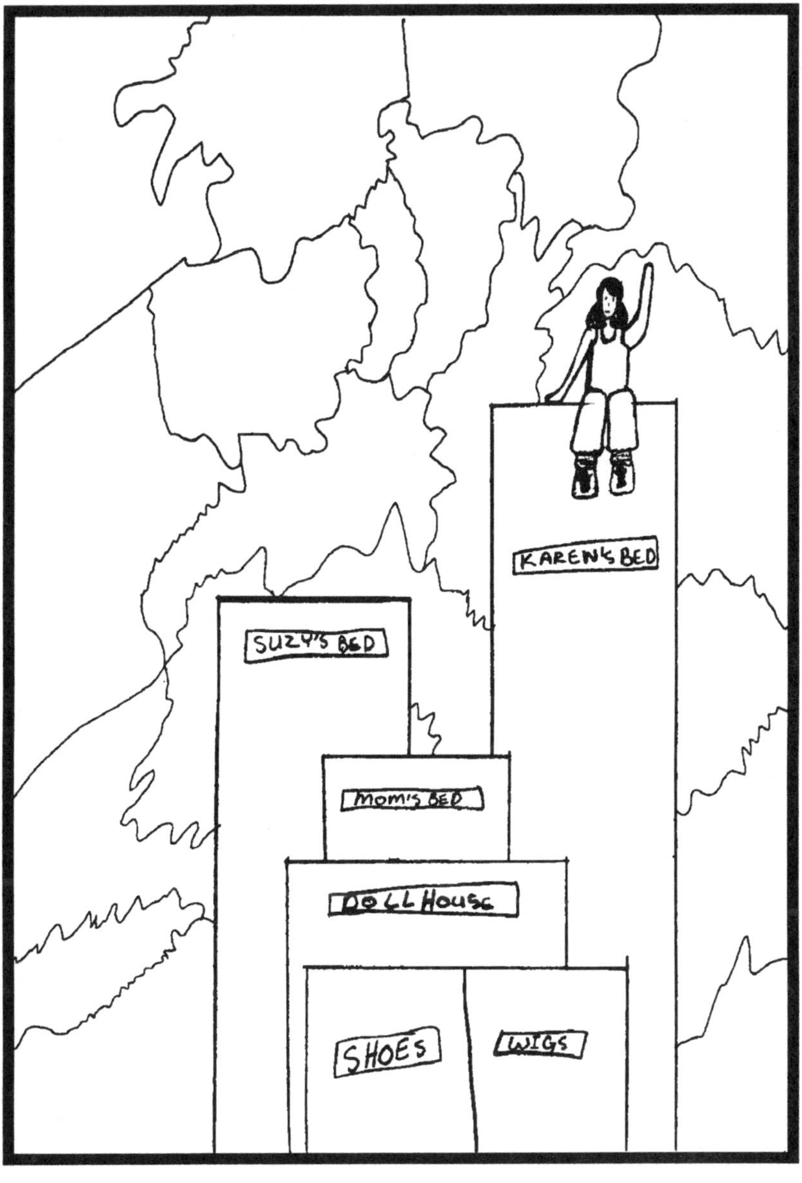
KAREN'S BED
SUZY'S BED
MOM'S BED
DOLLHOUSE
SHOES
WIGS

CHAPTER 1

How Do You Pack The Family's Feelings?

Two Families on the Move

The sudden news of the move burst upon the Johnson family like a late spring flood rolling down from the mountains and altering the lives of everyone in its path. Steve Johnson, an oil executive assigned to a Denver office, had long been concerned about his job in light of a company reorganization. When he finally received his official reassignment, his initial relief at keeping his position was offset by the bitter news that many of his close friends and colleagues were being terminated and that his office was being relocated to Houston within the month.

Steve's wife, Mary, had always known that relocation was a distinct possibility in Steve's business, however the sudden reality of uprooting their family, disrupting her sales career, and establishing a new home in a community a thousand miles away nearly overwhelmed her with anxiety and dread. Despite her own feelings of loss however, there was moving to be done. Though Mary and Steve hadn't discussed it, they both assumed that Mary was the one who was going to have to direct the move while Steve went ahead to his new office.

Laurie, the Johnson's eleven-year-old daughter, initially displayed an unexpected excitement about moving to a different city and living in a house with a swimming pool. She chattered incessantly about making new friends and attending a new school. In less enthusiastic moments, Laurie spent frequent quiet periods alone in her room or badgered her parents with endless queries about what the kids and schools and neighborhoods in the Houston area were like.

Karen, the Johnson's older daughter and a high school sophomore, outspokenly opposed the move from the instant she heard about it. She stormed about angrily, blaming her father and his company for forcing the family to move. She spent long, tearful sessions with friends she believed she would never see again. At one point she even threatened to run away and return to Denver if her parents forced her to move.

Now more than a year and a half later, the Johnsons are almost completely resettled physically and emotionally. Steve spent his first six months working long hours to reorganize his office staff and their operations and is just now starting to relax and spend more time with his family. Despite her own misgivings about relocating, Mary channeled her energy into finding and buying the right house and helping the kids get settled after the turmoil of moving. Only now is she finally taking steps to develop a local support system for herself as she contemplates resuming her career. As a couple Mary and Steve have just begun taking the time to assess the emotional effects of the move on their relationship.

Laurie's youthful enthusiasm for the move fluctuated almost daily with no apparent logic. After more than a few anxious moments when she first entered her new school, she made new friends, is now a star goalie on her soccer team, and can't wait to begin junior high school in the fall. Karen's first year in Houston was clearly the most difficult. She spent many tearful hours complaining to her parents about her unhappiness or making long distance phone calls to friends in Denver. Her grades dropped, and she often seemed depressed despite her apparent enjoyment of activities with her family. And only recently, after the intervention of an understanding high school counselor and the discovery of previously untapped acting skills that she utilized to join the drama club and debate team, has she allowed herself to let go of some of her sadness and see Houston as her new home.

* * * * *

For Darlene Stevens, a divorced mother of two, the decision to relocate came after many months of deliberate consideration. Following her divorce more than eight years earlier, Darlene had raised her two children Melissa, a college junior, and Brad, a sixth-grader, in a rural suburb of Colorado Springs. When Melissa entered Colorado State University, Darlene seriously began considering options for her own future and finally decided to move her family to Ft. Collins, Colorado where Melissa's school was located. She reasoned that because the cost of living in Ft. Collins would be significantly less, she could utilize the extra savings to return to school for a graduate degree and further her career.

Melissa greeted her mother's decision with unbridled enthusiasm. She had long encouraged Darlene to pursue a more rewarding position. The move also meant that she could be closer to her family and spend a great deal more time with them on weekends. With no doubts at all Melissa was ready to start helping her mother pack the moment she first heard the news.

Brad's reaction was a totally different story. He registered numerous complaints about his mother's plan. He didn't want to change schools. He didn't want to leave behind his close friends, his soccer team or his horse. He was certain that the new school would be inferior to his present one, that there were no kids his age in the community and that they certainly wouldn't have a soccer team. He also admitted that he was fearful that both his mother and sister would be so busy with school that neither would have any time to spend with him.

Darlene worked hard prior to the move to ease Brad's fears by taking him up to Ft. Collins, a distance of approximately 140 miles, for several weekend visits to investigate their new home and community. She arranged a day-long visit to his new school and scheduled an interview with the neighborhood soccer coach. Even more important, however, she spent a great deal of time talking with Brad about her own school and work schedule, her hopes for the move and the times she had planned to set aside for the family activities they could enjoy together.

The Stevens' move that summer was an excellent example of family teamwork in action with everyone pitching in to help. Now a year later Darlene, Melissa and Brad are all enrolled in and enjoying their respective school programs, and Brad is a starting center for the Cougars, which he enthusiastically describes as the best soccer team in Ft. Collins.

*   *   *   *   *

Every year, like explorers from times past, almost 41 million Americans like the Johnsons and the Stevens load their wagons and bravely follow their hearts down uncharted paths to new neighborhoods, far-away communities, different work places, unfamiliar schools, and at times exotic cultures and foreign lands. We move because families buy new homes, because parents change jobs, begin new careers, or perhaps separate and divorce. At times we move simply because life dictates that we grow up and advance to a new level of experience whether we're fully prepared for it or not. And as we set off on our new adventures and wave goodbye to friends and the familiarity of the past, it is likely that the very last carton we pack is the one labeled "family feelings."

Family moves often force changes that bring us face-to-face with the unfamiliar and the unexplored and cause emotional responses that can fluctuate from excitement one moment to uncertainty the next. As adults and parents, we sometimes grow so accustomed to accommodating life's changes we tend to forget that a family move can be a stressful as well as an exciting time for us and for our children. But if we look back at our own first moves, we can probably remember

How Do You Pack The Family's Feelings?

only too vividly the sentiments they provoked in us as youngsters.

While the adults packed cartons and prepared for moving day, we may have wondered why we had to move. We worried about whether we'd like our new homes and strange schools. We experienced sadness over leaving old friends and favorite haunts and questioned whether we'd ever be able to replace them. At times we felt apprehensive simply because moving was something we'd never done before, and we had no idea of what to expect from it.

For fleeting moments we may have visualized the move as an exciting adventure into the unknown with new sights to see, new things to do, new places to explore, and new friends to meet. But more than likely, we experienced a confusing jumble of feelings—anxiety, fear, sadness, anger, excitement and dread—that were difficult to understand, hard to express, and worst of all, impossible to control.

Now in adulthood we may handle moving more comfortably, but our children struggle with the same concerns we did when we first moved. It is important for us as parents to remember that confusion and uncertainty are normal reactions for all youngsters facing a move, just as they once were and perhaps still are for us.

Even more important to realize is that a move affects everyone in the family and that each family member may respond in different ways. A teenager, convinced that the move is some form of parental plot against adolescent happiness, may withdraw and act depressed or sullen, while an elementary school youngster may leap for joy at the thought of having her or his own room to decorate. A younger child may worry about the possibility of a favorite teddy bear or a cherished family mutt being left behind in an abandoned house. Parents may be too overwhelmed by the nightmare of carpet layers arriving two days after the movers or inlaws coming to visit before any boxes have been unpacked to notice that they haven't spoken a civil word to anyone or taken a moment for themselves since the phrase "moving day" became part of their vocabularies.

Naturally it would be marvelous if you could pack the family's feelings of comfort, familiarity, security and togetherness into one carton and move them from the old house to the new as easily as the furniture, garden tools and pots and pans. But adventures are never quite that simple.

The purpose of this book is to offer an effective method for putting the task of moving into manageable perspective. First we suggest that you try to perceive your move in distinct stages that require different skills and strategies as opposed to one overwhelming process that at times can seem wildly beyond your control. Imagine your move in three separate stages:

- The Preparation Stage
- The Work Stage
- The Settling-in Stage

In reality these stages may overlap, but viewing them as separate will allow you and your family to outline the necessary tasks for each stage and deal with your feelings about the move in a more enjoyable manner.

The Preparation Stage

The first stage of any move begins at the moment you realize that a move may occur and ends only when you have everyone and everything packed, loaded, and on the road. This stage entails the practical steps of house-hunting, house-selling, budgeting, financing, measuring and planning. It also includes the emotional steps of anticipation, excitement, waiting, worrying, and eventually saying goodbye to old friends and familiar places.

Moves occur for many reasons, and everyone in the family should have a clear understanding of the reason for a move. Families may decide they simply need more space or that

How Do You Pack The Family's Feelings?

they can finally afford the home of their dreams. A parent may be transferred to a job in a different community or decide to pursue a new career in a more promising area of the country. A marital separation, divorce, loss of a spouse, or significant financial setback may force a family to experience an unwanted move.

In the minds of most people, a voluntary move is usually greeted with more excitement and a greater sense of adventure than an involuntary and unforeseen one, which is often experienced as an intrusion into our lives. Unwanted moves may require families to confront more widespread emotional issues and greater feelings of loss than those related to a voluntary move. They may force families to confront relationship issues which had previously gone unnoticed, and they may force families to work harder to unify their energies in order to deal with the unwanted move.

The most important thing to remember, however, is that any life change carries with it both stresses and the potential for new experience. Personal growth and enjoyment are possible if you can resolve your reluctance to face the change. Even when a move is the result of a painful event, refocusing is an important step to take. Whatever the cause, whether the move is a chosen one or not, openly acknowledging the reasons for the move and refocusing on its positive opportunities are significant aspects of the Preparation Stage.

Another important point to keep in mind is that moves, like all significant life changes, tend to exaggerate existing family dynamics related to gender roles and responsibilities. For many families a familiar stereotype for a move is that the men load the rental truck while the women the pack the china, clean the cupboards and keep the children out of the way. Another, as in our example of the Johnson family, is the assumption that Dad will travel ahead to a new city to begin work while Mom stays behind with the kids to prepare for and execute the move. Automatic acceptance of such stereotypical gender roles creates a situation ripe for resentments and conflict long after the physical work of a move is completed.

Couples should not "assume" anything during times of transition. It is important that you discuss decisions, options and agreements openly in the context of how they will affect all members of the family. Examine old, reflexive roles, and leave yourselves open to creating new ways of working together.

Initially we had considered writing a chapter "for dads only". The assumption was that dads might take the time to read a chapter devoted to them but definitely would not read the entire book. We realized, however, that such a chapter could imply that the rest of the book and its suggestions regarding the moving process were the responsibility of moms.

We wish to make it clear, however, that this book is for everyone, the male and female members of the family. Moving is a family endeavor. Every person is essential to its success. Each stage of the moving process described in this book offers an opportunity to learn new ways of being with one another that honor each person's valuable contribution to the family. The true adventure of moving is that it creates a fertile time of change that allows movement and growth to occur in all areas of family life.

The Work Stage

The second stage of a move is the one with which we are probably all most familiar. This "cardboard box" stage of the move consists of the actual physical labor that includes cleaning, sorting, storing, wrapping, packing, junking, hauling and loading at one end and unpacking at the other.

There are two important things to remember during the Work Stage:

- ◆ Proper equipment, planning, preparation and predictability will make the move flow more smoothly and reduce the emotional and physical energy required of everyone.

- Every family member, including youngsters, should be actively involved so that they feel like an integral part of the moving process.

The Settling-in Stage

Though it is sometimes overlooked, the third and equally important part of a move is the process of getting acquainted with your new neighborhood and community.

Settling-in means:

- meeting neighbors,

- becoming familiar with new jobs and schools,

- dealing with the sadness of saying goodbye,

- overcoming anxieties and fears about your new setting,

- finding new "favorite" places,

- establishing new friendships.

Only when you've completed this stage can you call your new house a real home. Only then is your move really over.

As we mentioned earlier, moves normally carry with them feelings of excitement, hope, anticipation, stress, loss, fear, anger, and doubt. Even families whose entire lives are spent in a state of controlled transience such as military personnel or families whose financial livelihood depends on time-limited assignments and frequent transfers experience similar feelings. They may grow accustomed to the physical act of moving, but nothing really prepares them for the feelings that accompany those moves.

You can do yourself a great favor by recognizing and accepting that *all* of your feelings about the move including the negative or fearful ones are completely normal for anyone who has developed emotional ties to the people and places they enjoy. If you find yourself experiencing upsetting or disturbing feelings about your move, accept them simply as a sign of being fully human. Welcome them without self recrimination, criticism or guilt and realize that experiencing them and allowing them to dissipate on their own are necessary steps before moving on.

As parents, you can help your youngsters move most effectively by doing three things:

- Recall that confusing mix of emotions associated with your own childhood moves to help you understand what your kids may be experiencing.

- Realize that your children's feelings often reflect your own.

- And most important, taking the time to care for yourselves during the moving process so that you can maintain the physical and emotional energy level required to help your family enjoy the adventure that lies ahead.

With this self-awareness as a starting point, you can help heighten your family's enjoyment of the move by:

- Keeping your own stress levels to a minimum through planning, working together, setting aside personal relaxation time, sharing feelings and concerns, and giving each other support throughout all stages of the move.

- Creating predictability for your children by answering questions, providing schedules for various aspects of the move, and setting aside times for familiar family activities apart from the actual labor of moving.

- Fostering involvement of all family members by having them choose specific tasks they are willing to be responsible for, inviting family members to help make move-related decisions, and allowing children freedom to

unpack, arrange and decorate their own living areas in
your new home.

- Giving all family members adequate time and space to
unravel their own feelings about the move and to say
goodbye to those treasured people, places and things
they have left behind.

The chapters to follow offer hundreds of parent-child discussion topics, ideas for family activities, and practical tips to help make your move an enjoyable adventure in teamwork for your entire family.

A small note of caution about this book however: Just as moving can be an overwhelming process, so can trying to follow too many suggestions at the same time. For that reason we would like to suggest that you read only a few chapters at a time in order to allow yourself to reflect on your own feelings about the move and to consider which of these ideas will work best for you and your family. Relax, slow down and take some time as you travel these pages.

Good luck and happy moving!

Moving With Children

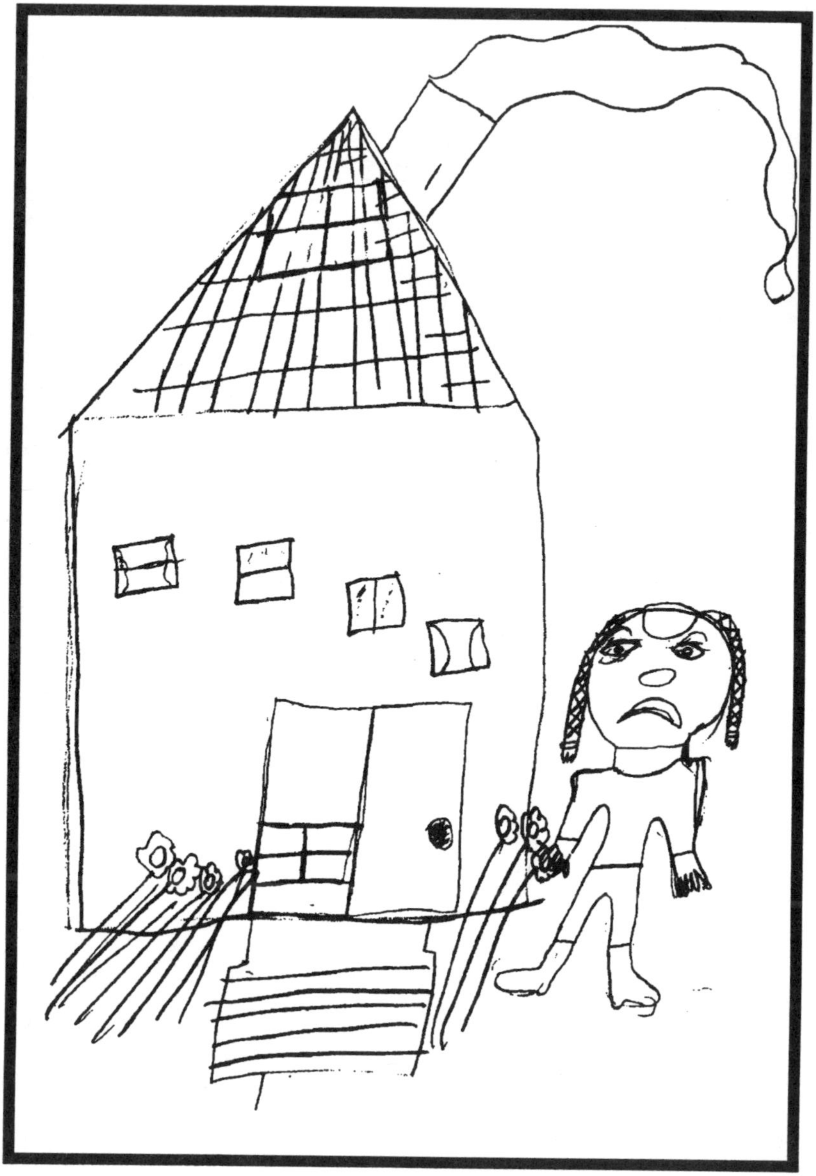

CHAPTER 2

Why Moving Causes Problems For Kids

Every year approximately 6 million kids across America move to new homes, neighborhoods and communities. For most of them moving can seem pretty scary. Despite the repeated reassurances of their parents, they question the reasons for the move, feel sadness about losing close friends and leaving behind familiar places, and worry about the unknown experiences that lie ahead. Even passing moments of excitement associated with the thoughts of a move as an adventure are mixed with feelings of anxiety, loss, anger and fear. These feelings are confusing for children because they can change from one moment to the next and are often at odds with the enthusiasm that other family members may exhibit about the move.

When you consider the number of significant changes that moving introduces into children's lives, it should not be at all surprising that kids don't express overwhelming enthusiasm when first confronted with the possibility of a family move. As a matter of fact, in a study by Kaoru Yamamoto, Ph.D., an educational psychologist from the University of Colorado at Denver, elementary school youngsters ranked moving to a new school as one of their 20 most stressful experiences (1). Furthermore, school-aged children who move to new homes experience the equivalent of 9 of the 43 items listed as possible stressors on The Social Readjustment Rating Scale (2).

To gain at least some understanding of the upsetting effects of moving, try this simple experiment with your family. Get everyone up early one morning, pack your car with all the clothing, snacks and supplies you may need for a full day of activity away from home, then drive to an unfamiliar part of the city or a neighboring community and spend the day doing errands, shopping, eating out, and entertaining your youngsters in places you have never seen before. When you return home that evening, you will have experienced a tiny but telling example of what lies ahead.

Now try for a few minutes to imagine the changes and emotional disruptions of everyday life brought about by the typical family move. One day children may be playing joyfully with close friends, succeeding comfortably in school, and feeling secure in the familiarity of a home and neighborhood which may be the only ones they have ever known, when parents, for no apparently logical or acceptable reason, place all this security, comfort, and feeling of achievement in jeopardy with the announcement that the family is going to move. To make matters worse, the statements "We're not quite sure when" and "We haven't really decided where" are sometimes tacked on to the end of the moving proclamation.

Following this parental declaration, the first words out of a child's mouth, much to a parent's chagrin, may be, "Why do we have to move? I like it here. I don't want to move!" Needless to say, if parents have mixed feelings about relocating or if the move is a forced or unwanted one, the family's moving adventure has already begun on emotionally shaky ground.

Beyond a mere lack of enthusiasm, an often-employed kid strategy at this point is to ignore the parents' announcement about the move, as though ignoring the move will somehow keep it from occurring. Some children, usually pre-teens and teenagers, will carry this strategy to the extremes of not cooperating in keeping the house clean while it is on the mar-

Why Moving Causes Problems For Kids

ket, refusing to become involved in preparing or packing for the move, or formulating elaborate plans to live with neighbors or a best friend as the rest of the family waves goodbye from the back of the moving van.

On a recent trip to Bozeman, MT one of the authors overheard a slightly more subtle twist on this same strategy employed by a clever nine-year-old youngster named Jake. The following conversation between Jake and his mother, Susie, resulted from a passing comment she had made about having given some thought to moving.

Susie: "During the last couple of months I've been thinking of getting a place a little closer to town."

Jake: "Why do you want to do that, Mom?"

Susie: "Because it's quite a drive from our house to town, Jake."

Jake: "That's no reason to move, Mom."

Susie: "That's not the only reason, Jacob. Our house is pretty big, and it takes a lot of work to keep it up."

Jake: "No it doesn't, Mom. It doesn't take any work at all."

Susie: "Well, you might think so because you don't have to do any of it."

Jake: "But I would. I promise if we don't move, I'll do all of the work around the house. But if we move, I'm not doing anything!"

Along with the vague uncertainties of "When are we moving?" "Where are we going to live?" and "What will become of us?" come more immediate anxieties and disruptions to the family routine. Regardless of the distance involved in a move, whether it's from New York City to San Francisco or simply to a home in a neighboring subdivision, one or both parents must frequently devote sizable chunks of time to meeting with realtors, negotiating with builders, or simply driving around various neighborhoods in search of the "perfect" house. The financial realities of what the family would like and what they can afford along with the children's growing restlessness during the search process often add to the family's burden. As each day passes without observable or acceptable progress, adult frustrations, doubts, and anxieties typically increase.

As parental tension mounts, children—especially younger ones—become increasingly aware of receiving less time and attention from mom and dad, which can affect their sense of comfort and security. Kids in this situation often begin to play detective in the hopes of picking up clues about what might be happening and not infrequently blame themselves for the family's discomfort and tension and sometimes for the move itself.

Margaret, a woman attending one of our parent workshops, shared a touching story about her first move that exemplifies this tendency of children beautifully.

As a third-grader Margaret had suffered from learning disabilities which caused her significant academic difficulties and emotional upset during the school year. That summer her parents bought a larger home, and the family moved to a new neighborhood which also required that Margaret and her sisters transfer to a new school. For more than fifteen years, Margaret was convinced that the move was the result of the family's disappointment and shame at her poor third grade school performance. Later as a graduate student Margaret shared this long-held secret fear with her mother. She was both shocked and relieved when her mother gave her a tearful hug and told her that she and Margaret's father had decided on that move so many years before so each of the girls could have a bedroom of their own.

Another factor adding to the family's stress level is the disruption of familiar and comfortable routines prior to the sale of their house. Instead of flopping in front of the television for dinner or dropping toys and clothes on the bedroom floor, kids are now under strict orders to keep the house neat

Why Moving Causes Problems For Kids

in case someone wants to see it on short notice. What used to be quiet evenings at home for children and parents are now spent with one ear cocked for the telephone in fear of an unexpected visit from a realtor and a potential buyer. Lazy weekends of relaxing or gardening in the yard are replaced by having to be away from home for several hours each Saturday and Sunday so the realtor can hold an open house.

An equally disruptive and sometimes frightening event for children are the frequent comings and goings of strangers in their home before its sale. The presence of real estate agents, potential buyers, appraisers, workmen and, worst of all, other children coming to look at the house with their parents can contribute to your child's feelings of a loss of privacy, security, comfort and identity at the very time that she or he is struggling to say goodbye to close friends and neighbors that will be left behind.

Further along in the preparation stage of your move, the discomfort and complexity of carrying on daily routines under packing conditions add to everyone's insecurity level as moving day draws nearer. More and more loaded cartons line the walls and fewer and fewer household items appear in their normal places, not to mention the ever-diminishing amounts of time for fun family activities. One piece of good news, however, is that many families discover that the memories of this disrupted premove life-style motivate some children to keep their rooms in a new house picked up and neat for almost an *entire week* following a family move!

Finally, as the realities of moving day become more evident, it is not uncommon for a child's sense of loss, fear of the unknown, and uncertainty about a move to be expressed in more dramatic ways through tearfulness, fears, or withdrawal. These responses are often triggered by the irrefutable evidence—stacked cartons. empty rooms or the arrival of movers—that the move is actually going to occur despite the child's fondest wishes that the whole notion of moving would soon be abandoned.

Several youngsters with whom we have worked in therapy because of difficulties in dealing with family moves can serve as examples. Patrick, the eleven-year-old son of a widowed mother facing a move to a new community, expressed repeated fears that both his mother and older sister would find new jobs, move away, and abandon him to live on his own. Brandi, a ten-year-old girl, experienced nightmares about her new home's developing cracks in the basement walls that would suddenly cause it to crumble after the family moved in. And Kevin, an eight-year-old boy, attempted to sabotage his family's moving day by hiding in the basement of his old home in the belief that his parents would cancel the move if they couldn't find him when the movers arrived.

At moving time it is extremely important for parents to realize that these feelings are natural for all kids and that they usually become more manageable as the family becomes more acquainted with their new home and neighborhood. Until that post-move period of adjustment is completed, however, most adult reassurances that "everything will be fine" are likely to go unheeded by youngsters whose sentiments are in direct conflict with parental logic.

In many ways the stages of a child's reaction to the realities of moving are similar to those of patients confronting a terminal illness (3).

- Initially a child will deny the reality of a move and continue to function as if it were not something she or he has to deal with, regardless of what the rest of the family does.

- As parental behavior reinforces the idea that the move is imminent, a child may become angry, balky or defiant.

- A third stage for some children, as evidenced in our young friend Jacob, is an attempt to negotiate or bargain with parents to keep from moving.

- The fourth stage is one of resignation and sadness when the child begins to experience losses associated with a move.

- The fifth and final stage, which also signals the stirrings of a new beginning, is the acceptance of the move as a fact of life and an active interest in exploring the family's new surroundings.

To help summarize the many elements of a move that can cause stress for children and to understand youngsters' possible emotional reactions to these stressors, we have broken them down according to the three stages of a move. Simply being aware of what stage of the move your family is facing and which stressors may be present can help defuse some of the emotional hardship your youngsters may be experiencing (4).

Potential Preparation Stage Stressors on Children

- The unpredictability of the moving schedule

- The presence of strangers in the house

- The disruption of familiar family routines and activities

- Reduced time and attention and possible periods of separation from parents

- Unaccustomed travel to visit a new neighborhood or community prior to the move

- The process of having to break the news and answer questions about the move to friends, classmates and neighbors

Children's Emotional Responses to Preparation Stage Stressors

- Mood swings and insecurity related to the unpredictability of the moving schedule and concerns and fantasies about the unknown

- Concerns about the reasons for the move

- Anxieties related to the disruption of family schedules, reduced time and attention and possible separation from parents

- Concerns about the presence of strangers in the house

- Feelings of anger and loss of control about being forced to move, primarily in older children and adolescents

- Sadness and feelings of loss about saying goodbye

Many of the stressors introduced into children's lives during the Preparation Stage will persist until your move is completed, but the Work and Settling-in stages bring additional stressors of their own.

Potential Work Stage Stressors on Children

- The disruption of a comfortable family structure

- The physical demands of packing and cleaning

- The necessity of giving away or leaving behind familiar belongings

- Physically leaving friends and neighbors

- The excitement, disruption and physical labor of moving day

- The possible rigors of traveling to a new home

Children's Emotional Responses to Work Stage Stressors

- Discomfort and stress caused by the physical disruption of the home

- Fears of valued possessions, pets and family members being left behind

- Sadness and loss at leaving friends and neighbors

- Fears of becoming lost or separated from parents and family

- Concerns and fears about travel to a strange community

Potential Settling-in Stage Stressors on Children

- The possible delay, loss or damage to possessions during the move

- The physical demands of unpacking, storing and decorating

- The work of making home comfortable

- The re-establishment of familiar family routines and schedules

- The absence of a familiar support group

- The process of becoming acquainted with a new community and meeting new neighbors

Children's Emotional Responses to Settling-in Stage Stressors

- Discomfort and stress caused by an unfamiliar place and disrupted family routines

- Sadness or anger at the loss of or damage to valued belongings

- Concerns and fears about exploring a new neighborhood or school and possibly becoming lost

- Feelings of isolation, shyness or loss of status (particularly among adolescents) in a new community

- Worries about being accepted and fitting in

- Continued sadness about having left friends or a family member

*   *   *   *   *

Parents may not observe all of these emotional responses in any one youngster since each child will respond in her or his own way. In some cases parents may not even realize that a youngster is responding to a specific stressor because of that child's manner of coping with stress. There are, however, several simple steps you can take to help your children better understand their mixed emotions about your impending move.

1. *Try to be aware of the verbal and behavioral signals your children may be sending that reflect their feelings about the move.*

Verbally, youngsters may voice complaints about your choice of homes, the neighborhood or community, the school they will attend, or other children on the block. They may express dissatisfaction or anger with present friends as a way of creating an emotional distance to help lessen their feelings of loss. They may begin to ask unexpected questions or make random comments about your new home, or they may begin to express fears that seem new and illogical in the context of their usual emotional moods.

Behaviorally, youngsters may become quiet and withdrawn, less active, negative, angry or fearful. They may experience sleeplessness or nightmares; or they might exhibit a drop in school performance, a loss of interest in previously enjoyed activities, or a reluctance to leave home or to spend time away from the family.

All of these verbal and behavioral cues are common indicators of a child's inner struggle to deal with the intense and often confusing feelings associated with a move. By being aware of these signals, parents can use them to focus discussions on the feelings children may be grappling with in relation to the move. The following list summarizes the various indicators that a child may be experiencing undue levels of stress that might require greater parental attention (5).

Signs of Move-related Stress in Children

- Anger and conflict with friends, siblings or parents
- New and illogical fears
- Reluctance to be apart from home or family
- Loss of interest in previously enjoyed activities
- Drop in school performance
- Refusal to cooperate in preparing for the move
- Denial about the reality of the move
- Refusal to discuss the move
- Unusual or more frequent temper tantrums

- Excessive negativism, sadness or inappropriate crying

- Helplessness or regression in younger children

- Sleep difficulties, nightmares or bed-wetting

- Excessive worry about the new school and neighborhood

- Excessive and groundless complaints about the new school or neighborhood

2. *Reassure your children that whatever thoughts and feelings they may be having, regardless of how critical, painful or scary, these are normal and natural for anyone facing a move.*

Demonstrating your willingness to discuss these feelings with your children in an accepting, noncritical manner will encourage them to share their feelings more openly. Such discussion will offer you the opportunity to reassure your kids not that "everything will be fine" but that given some time, their feelings about your new home may eventually change.

In this process you will also discover that simply offering youngsters the opportunity to talk about their anger, fears and anxieties openly will reduce the intensity of these negative feelings and increase your children's willingness to view the move in a more positive light.

3. *Keep in mind that, as a parent, you are a powerful role model for your children, and they will look to you for cues as to how they should react to the prospects of moving.*

If you are excited and confident about the move, it is likely that they will be, too. On the other hand if you are operating under a high level of stress or anxiety, your kids will mirror this tension as well.

Children often wonder, and sometimes worry, about what their parents may be thinking and feeling. Sharing some of your own feelings of loss, uncertainty, sadness and concern about the move offers children another perspective against which to measure their own uncertain emotions and gives them the message that it is acceptable to discuss conflicting feelings openly in the family. For a family whose move is precipitated by a divorce or the death of a family member, these truth-telling conversations also offer healing to the feelings accompanying such a loss.

Furthermore, children enjoy hearing about what parents faced when they were kids, since it offers them possible new ideas for solving their own childhood dilemmas. Recalling some of your reactions to your first childhood move can provide you an excellent insight into what your children may be experiencing, and sharing these memories can reassure them that you understand their present feelings.

4. Finally, when all other sources of expertise seem to have failed, remember that children are always intrigued by how other youngsters in similar situations have felt about and resolved their difficulties.

For this reason we have devoted Chapter 3 to some of the responses of more than 2,500 children who shared with us their thoughts and feelings about moving as well as practical tips and suggestions for getting acquainted in unfamiliar neighborhoods, adjusting to new schools, meeting people and making new friends.

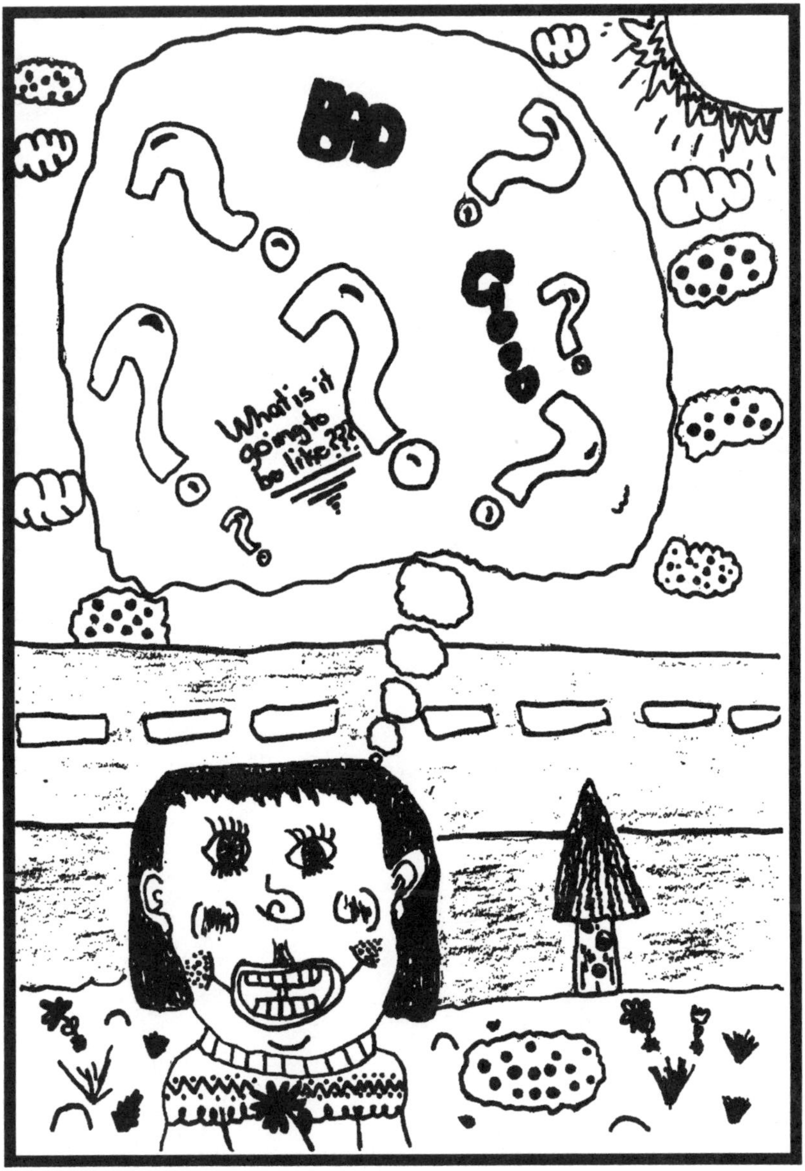
BAD
GOOD
What is it going to be like???

CHAPTER 3

How Kids Feel About Moving

To gain a clearer understanding of how children really feel about moving, we surveyed approximately 2,500 elementary and middle school youngsters. In this chapter we share a sampling of their responses to the question, "What kinds of things did you think about and what kinds of feelings did you have when you moved to a new school or neighborhood?" Their comments offer a starting place for discussing the different emotions your own children may be experiencing as your move becomes imminent.

What Kids Have to Say About Moving

"When I moved to a different neighborhood, I worried that I wouldn't have as many people around that I knew. I was also afraid because I'd never moved before and I didn't know what to expect from it." –Kenny, 6th Grade

"I have never moved to a new school, but I moved to a new neighborhood when I was five. It was hard. I had a friend named Josh, and we played together a lot. When we moved, I didn't see him much, actually hardly at all. I didn't like it at first, but then I met a lot of people. I hope we never move again, well, at least for a while." –Sarah, 5th Grade

"When I moved to a new school, I thought it would be hard to make new friends and get to know the school. And I was afraid that school would be too hard." –Cammie, 4th Grade

"I moved three times. I was born in Missouri and then moved to Denver. When I moved to my new school, it was scary at first because I only knew two people. So every night I would be really scared because I didn't like school and didn't know anybody." –Jel, 5th Grade

"If I moved, I would be mad about leaving and happy to meet new friends." –Matt, 3rd Grade

"When we moved to a new neighborhood, the two questions I thought about most were, 'Are they going to like me?' and 'Am I going to like them?'" –Damian, 5th Grade

"If you move to a new school and a new house, you hate your new house at first, but you get used to it. And I think school is bad because you don't know anybody, and you don't know how to act." –Billy, 3rd Grade

"When I switched schools from St. Ann's School to Aikahi, I felt scared because I thought I might not make any new friends, but it wasn't too bad after all." –Katrina, 5th Grade

"When I moved here from Alaska, I felt strange because it was totally different. I had more chores and I felt kind of pressured. And sometimes I cried because I got homesick." –Jessica, 4th Grade

"I moved to a new school once, and I was excited because I could meet new people. But I was also nervous because I didn't know if anyone would like me." –James, 5th Grade

I moved to Hawaii from a country in Africa. I was sad to leave my friends and my old school, and I was scared because I didn't know English." –Jimmy, 5th Grade

"I was scared at first going to a new school and all. I was afraid the big kids would lock me in my locker. And I was scared that I wouldn't be able to find my way around. But I was excited to go to a new school." –Alicia, 6th Grade

"When I moved, I felt lonely at first because everyone else had friends and I didn't." –Tanya, 5th Grade

How Kids Feel About Moving

"I have not moved to a new school, but if I did, I would feel like I was in a different world. I would feel like I was always being stared at. I'd want to make a friend as soon as possible." –Heather, 4th Grade

"When I moved, I wondered what it would be like to live in a new city and what the other kids would be like." –Matt, 5th Grade

"I haven't moved, but I would probably think about trying to make new friends and not worry about the friends where I used to live. My feelings would be mixed up because I would have to change to the new school rules." –Stephen, 5th Grade

"When I moved, I was only a baby. If I moved now, I'd probably be sad about moving away from my friends. But I'd be happy too because it would be a new experience, hopefully fun. I would get a chance to meet new people and make new friends. I love to meet new people." –Jenny, 6th Grade

"When I moved to a new neighborhood, most of the time I thought about how much I would miss my friends and how much I liked my old teachers. Sometimes I would worry about other kids not liking me or having mean teachers, but it turned out that I was wrong." –Sally, 4th Grade

"I have moved many times, and I always think about what if the kids at school don't like me. But I know that it's usually fine." –Jami, 4th Grade

"I've moved to a new house and a new school. It was very exciting and a very nervous time in my life. It's frightening but happy too. I enjoy moving." –Mark, 5th Grade

"When I moved to Colorado Springs, my first house and school were a lot different, but the people were kind. At school people offered to take me around, and they introduced me to the other kids who became my friends. Our next house and school were easier because even before we bought the house, I found a friend next door. A man in his yard said that he had a son in the fourth grade who introduced me to the kids at school." –David, 4th Grade

"I'm going to be moving to New Jersey soon so this is probably going to help me get ideas on how to make friends. What I'm going to do is just try to fit in with the other kids and do the stuff they do. And I will try to be nice to them and help them when they need help." –Cory, 5th Grade

Discussion Tips for Parents

As you can see, children experience a variety of conflicting emotions at the time of a move, so when you set out to discover how your children feel about moving, a few simple parent/child discussion guidelines may prove helpful.

First, remember that most children aren't accustomed to sitting down and discussing issues with adults for long periods of time. So look for natural opportunities to interject comments or questions regarding the move into your daily activities. Keep the discussions short and in line with your child's typical attention span.

To encourage your child's willingness to express feelings about the move, be sure to talk with her or him about your own. You might read some of the responses from our "kid experts" in this chapter and ask if your youngster has had similar thoughts or emotions, or you could choose the quotes that reflect how each of you might be feeling and discuss these with personal examples that fit for your family.

If your child is of reading age, have her or him look through the list and share with you some of the comments that best reflect how she or he might be feeling. An enjoyable family activity to stimulate discussion is to have each member of the family choose the "kid expert" who best expresses her or his own feelings about the move and then discuss your feelings as a group.

Kids' Questions About Moving

If you're not quite certain how to begin talking to children about a move, the following list of commonly-asked questions is a good place to begin (6).

- Why do we have to move?
- Where will we live?
- When are we moving?
- Will I ever see my friends again?
- What will our new house be like?
- Will we know anyone at our new house?
- Will there be any kids my age at our new house?
- What will the kids be like in our new neighborhood?
- What if the kids there make fun of me?
- What if nobody likes me?
- What school will I go to?
- Will my school be harder than the one I go to now?
- What will my teacher be like?
- What if I can't find my way around school?
- What if I get lost?

There is one other frequently asked question we have deliberately left off the list because we feel it deserves special attention. That question is: Can we move back if we don't like our new house? Often children who have concerns and anxieties about a move will try to gain some reassurance from parents that moving home is always an option if things don't work out as they would like. The simple answer in almost all cases is *no*.

There are times, especially when a child is extremely upset by the thought of moving, that parents are tempted to respond with a "yes" or "We'll see." in an effort to comfort the youngster or to avoid dealing with the child's upset directly. This strategy usually leads to trouble simply because there are very few, if any, families who can afford the luxury of moving back for any reason at all.

By assuring a youngster that returning to a former home is a possibility, parents set up unrealistic expectations for children that can lead them to put their adjustment efforts on hold and wait out the move until the time comes to return home. An even more disturbing possibility is that such false reassurance may actually cause some children to behave in a manner that creates unhappiness in misdirected attempts to speed their return to a former home. In either situation the emotional results of such a parental miscommunication are more disturbing for the family than a simple but truthful "no" in the first place.

Finally, don't be surprised if your child's initial response to the thought of moving is a negative one and don't feel pressured to convince your child that the move will have positive outcomes. *Your task is simply to allow youngsters the opportunity to express their feelings openly without having to justify or defend them.* This will allow them to adjust to the move at their own personal pace and, later, begin to evaluate it in a more positive light.

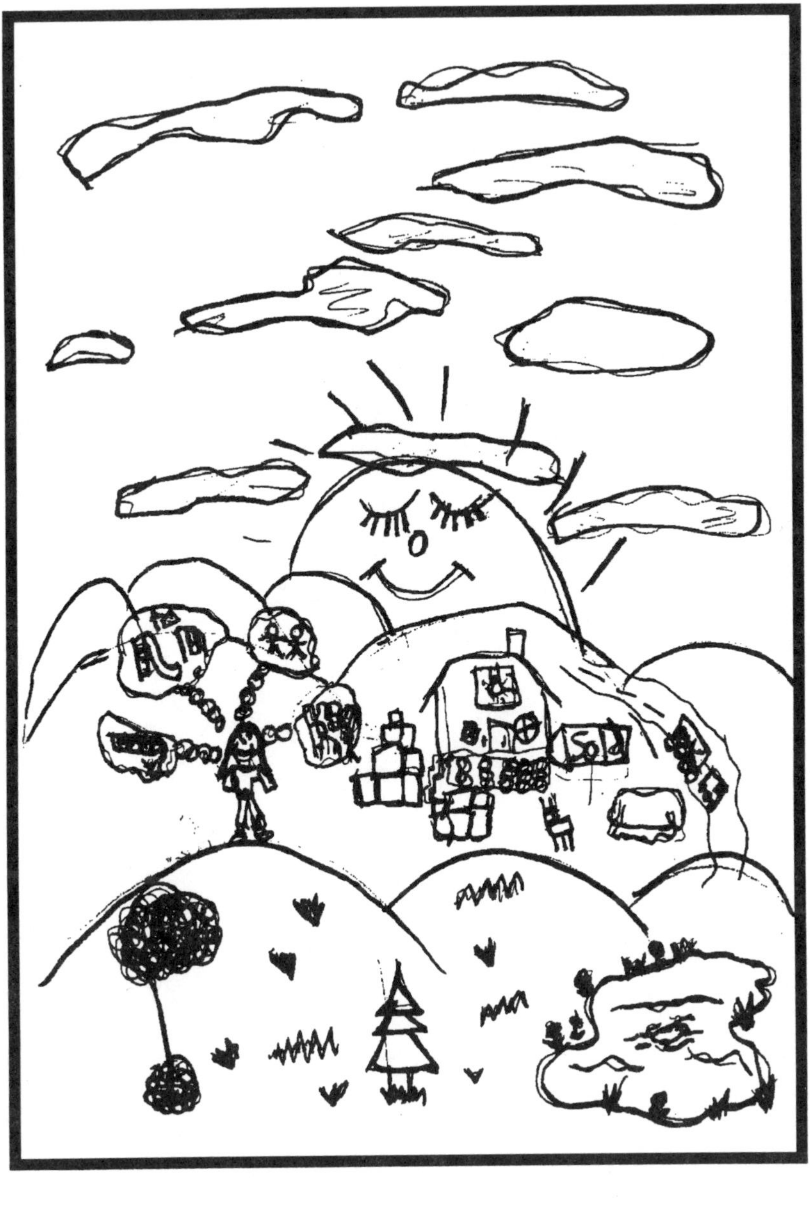
Sold

CHAPTER 4

When You Move Matters (Sometimes)

Regardless of when and how well you plan your move, it is only realistic to anticipate that the relocation process will probably not go exactly as scheduled and will most likely cause some emotional disruption for everyone in the family. In the real world you will find that home sales, bank loans, real estate closings, builders' schedules, apartment leases, moving companies and job transfers rarely operate on wholly predictable timetables. These can cause chaos even in the best of moving plans.

One of the authors still remembers his family's first move when he was in the third grade. Originally scheduled for late August, the move was postponed several times because of construction delays. Each week as he reappeared in his usual seat in the classroom, teachers and classmates greeted him with a repetitive barrage of questions and comments: "I thought you were moving." "Why haven't you moved yet?" "When are you moving?" For an eight-year-old the answers became slightly more difficult each week, and final good-byes were never made, for the move finally occurred suddenly and with little notice.

When you contemplate the best time for your family move in terms of your children's emotional adjustment, the answer is fairly simple (yet complex): "There is no best time for a family move, but some times are better than others."

Being realistic, you can expect that whenever the move, your family will experience some degree of emotional upheaval. You can, however, avert complete family disasters by *never* moving on Thanksgiving or Christmas Day, your child's birthday, Super Bowl Sunday, or on your wedding anniversary if you can avoid it. The ease of moving at any other times of the year depends on many factors, including your children's ages, their grade levels in school, the extent of their involvement in organized activities, and the amount of teamwork your family has created in working toward the move.

For preschool children, who react most strongly to change, special dates and predictability of schedules hold far less importance than familiarity and a sense of security. Their reactions to a move will be based not on when you move but upon their perceptions of continuity and the reassurance that the essentials of family life will not change significantly as a result of the move. For these youngsters a parent's reassurances that focus on the safe arrival of a child's favorite toys, clothing, furniture, room decorations, pets, and all members of the family at your new home will prove most effective.

For these same reasons, moves that require relocating a family in stages, often as a result of a job transfer or a divorce, are more difficult for younger children because of one parent's extended absence. If a move must be made in stages, the family should strive to maintain regular contact between children and the absent parent by phone and mail. Frequent reassurances to these youngsters about the safety of absent family members are also important to their sense of security.

For school-aged youngsters of approximately 5 to 13 years of age, the question of when to schedule a family move is slightly more complex. Children within this age group are still centered around the family for their sense of identity and security and are often most comfortable in dealing with a move as long as their basic sense of family remains intact.

Older youngsters within this age range who are beginning to examine their independence outside of the family boundaries are more likely to struggle with questions about fitting in to a new classroom, concerns about being able to meet the academic demands of an unfamiliar school, or the disruption of missing out on organized activities which they enjoy.

Moving is most difficult for adolescents between the ages of 14 and 18 whose primary developmental task is to establish an identity independent of their family's (7). Often they have developed close relationships with friends, loyalties to sports teams, clubs or part time jobs, and may be experiencing the first stirrings of adolescent romance, all of which seem doomed by the family's move. For these reasons parents should not find it surprising that teenagers resist relocation most strenuously. One rather obvious response to the question about the best time for a family move is simply, "not during high school."

When a move must occur regardless of children's ages, however, the general scheduling question becomes whether it is best to move during the school year or over the course of the summer. The answer, like most responses to seemingly simple questions, is, "It depends."

Moving during the summer provides many positives because families have more time to prepare for a move, children can spend leisure time with friends and remain in activities they enjoy, and goodbyes become more natural because friends will be leaving on vacations, traveling to visit relatives, or attending summer camps. Families who complete a move during the summer also have more time to become acquainted with a new neighborhood before children enter school in September.

On the other hand, unless parents plan far enough ahead, they may find that a summer move has not allowed them ample time to investigate organized summer activities and that they are now stranded with a houseful of bored youngsters complaining there is nothing to do. Another reality about summer moves is that children in many neighborhoods enroll in summer activities, travel, attend camps, and visit relatives so there is a possibility that few neighborhood kids will be available for your child to get acquainted with.

Another word of caution expressed by our "kid experts" about summer moves is the disheartening possibility of investing time and energy into establishing a friendship with another child in the neighborhood only to discover that she or he is a mere visitor living with a divorced parent for the summer or, worse, the discovery once school begins that the new friend is an outcast among her or his classmates.

A move during a school year presents a different set of concerns for most children, primarily the multiple burden of having to adjust to an unfamiliar classroom, trying to establish new friendships, and getting settled at home all at the same time. On the positive side, changing schools early in the fall or during a natural pause in the academic year such as spring break often allows a classroom teacher more time to devote to helping a new student become familiar with classroom procedures and fellow classmates.

Without a doubt, having youngsters enter a new school in late spring, April or May, can cause the most potential difficulty because it forces a child to fit into a setting where teachers and students alike are already looking forward to getting out of school and are not likely to invest a great deal of energy into helping a new youngster adjust to the classroom.

The consensus of educational experts cited by Denver's Piton Foundation (8) indicates that moving during the summer is less harmful to youngsters academically than a move during the school year. In the experience of the authors, the least disruptive time for a child to undergo a move seems to be a few weeks before the start of an academic year because it allows children enough time to explore new neighborhood

When You Move Matters (Sometimes)

surroundings and still begin the school year when other youngsters are becoming acquainted with new teachers, classroom rules, and academic expectations for the very first time. This timing reduces a child's concern of having to adjust to a system that everyone else already seems to know, and the beginning of the school year is the most likely time for teachers to plan get-acquainted activities for the entire class and to have extra time and energy to devote to new students.

Again, the reality of relocating is simply that you may not be able to choose exactly when you move; but keep in mind that working together as a family, offering support and reassurance to one another, and sharing concerns, feelings and a sense of adventure can overcome many of the difficulties that poor timing may present. Or to paraphrase our earlier response to the question regarding the best time for a family move, the answer is, "There is no best time for a family move, but in a loving, supportive family any time can be a good one."

When You Talk About Moving Matters

A much simpler though equally important scheduling matter is when to tell children about an impending move. Although there may not be a perfect time, parents should never try to conceal the family's intention to move or to surprise youngsters in the hope of sparing them from emotional turmoil. Children can be curiously telepathic with their parents. They can pick up on the slightest emotional and physical cues that a change is in the wind. Trying to keep a move a secret causes a sense of emotional discontinuity and can result in outcomes far more disruptive than those the parents wished to avoid. Therefore, as we all learned as kids, truth is the best policy.

An extreme but telling example of such a case is that of Robbie, who had gone to visit his grandparents for the summer. When he returned, he discovered that his parents had moved into a new house while he was away. They had assumed that he would be excited about coming back to a new home and that the move would be easier without him under foot. Unfortunately Robbie spent many months of uneasiness in his new house and neighborhood before really becoming comfortable there, and he experienced fear whenever he was separated from his parents for any length of time as a result of their moving plan.

Children need time to adjust to the idea of moving, and they deal best with their feelings by having repeated opportunities to talk about them. A general but effective rule for parents is: *When you announce the news of a move, give children ample notice to allow them to talk about the move and say goodbye to their friends.*

Preschool-aged youngsters developmentally lack an accurate perception of time as well as a clear understanding of what a move entails. In talking with them, parents should give themselves at least six weeks to explain in simple, understandable terms what the move will mean for the family and the child. School-aged youngsters with a better understanding of the concept of moving should be given at least eight weeks notice or longer, especially if preparations for the move are clearly evident and affecting the family's everyday life. Older children and adolescents whose lives may be more greatly affected by the news and who will be more actively involved in the move itself should be told as soon as possible.

Giving children this advance notice and clear understanding about the move allows them the opportunity to express their negative feelings and deal with some of their uncertainties and fears prior to the move. Then, when moving day finally does arrive, hopefully you and the kids can turn your positive energies into making the move the beginning of a new adventure.

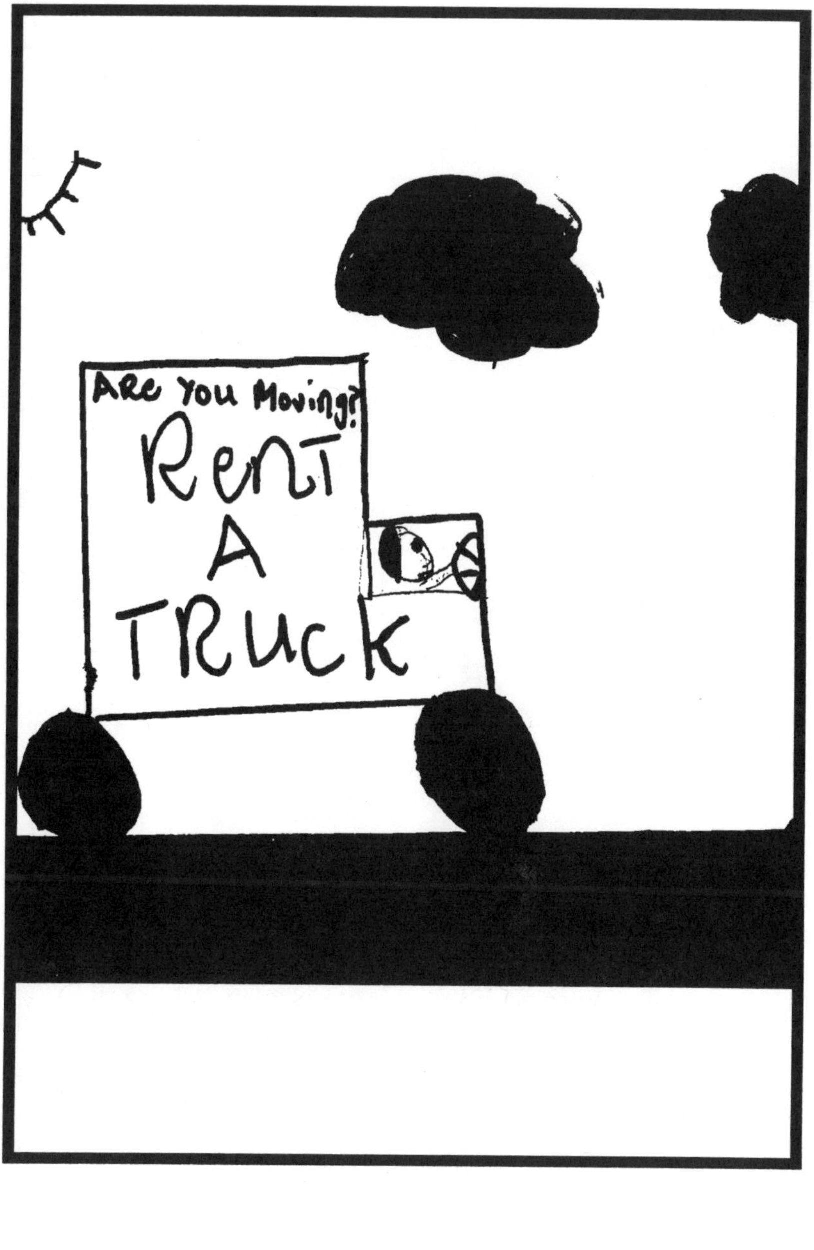
Are You Moving?
Rent
A
TRUCK

CHAPTER 5

Practical Moving Tools For Families

As we mentioned in Chapter 1, your family's moving adventure begins at the moment you first realize that a move may occur, usually long before you have packed even one carton. It ends only when your family is settled in a new home, familiar and comfortable with your new surroundings, and putting down roots by making friends and discovering new "favorite" places to call your very own. As in any major project, careful planning, realistic scheduling, teamwork and the proper set of equipment will help produce results that are satisfying for everyone.

To accomplish this end, it is important to keep a few, basic organizing principles in mind.

- Everyone in the family should be actively involved in the move, and each member of the family, including youngsters, should be assigned tasks for which they are responsible.

- About six to eight weeks before your move, creating a calendar or schedule will help keep everyone organized and provide a sense of predictability for your children.

- Making moving chores fun and working together as a group will contribute to everyone's sense of involvement, reduce family stress, and produce greater work enjoyment. All of this will ultimately result in an easier move.

- The process of moving, in itself, can be an exhausting one, so be sure to schedule times for family fun and relaxation.

- Like any job moving requires a proper set of equipment.

In this chapter, we would like to share some practical tools that have proven to be useful for families on the move. We invite you to use your family's imagination to utilize our suggestions or to create your own unique set of "moving tools."

Premove Supplies for Kids

Much to their dismay parents often discover that the six to eight weeks of preparation time they thought they had prior to moving day have been gobbled up by a combination of the many required daily duties—those tasks associated with house hunting, buying, selling, leasing, renting, cleaning, packing, storing and hauling—and the day-to-day crises which inevitably arise when families with children are involved in a move. An effective means of encouraging family cooperation and reducing "kid crisis time" is to provide each of your children with a set of premoving supplies suitable to the child's interests, age and ability level. Some helpful things to include in your child's premove equipment package are:

- a set of colored pens, markers, or pencils, a colorful pad of paper, and a set of envelopes for kids to write goodbye notes, make moving lists, or do drawings of your old home
(They can also be useful for making *"PLEASE DO NOT TOUCH"* signs for your kids to put on their favorite toys, models, school projects, stereos, video games, etc. when your home is being shown to potential buyers who may have children of their own.)

Practical Moving Tools For Families

- a small address or autograph book for your kids to collect autographs, personal messages, addresses and phone numbers from friends

- a scrapbook or photo album for each child's photographs, drawings and mementos of your old home and neighborhood

- a packet of pre-addressed postcards with your new address for your children to hand out to friends

- a packet of blank postcards pre-addressed by each of your child's friends so your kids can write to them easily after the move

- a book of stamps so your children can send postcards or notes to friends or relatives during or immediately after the move

- an inexpensive pocket camera and a few rolls of film so your children can take photographs of your old neighborhood or friends and classmates

- a photograph of your new home for your kids to share with friends and classmates

- a map of your new community or neighborhood

- a floor plan of your new home so you can discuss various decorating decisions with your children

- a floor plan of each child's room with dimensions so they can begin thinking about furniture placement and decoration

- a packet of address change cards from the post office so your children can begin receiving their favorite magazines as soon as possible

- a moving guide or travel packet for kids from your moving company

- a Premove Checklist (see example, Page 53) of things to be done by your kids prior to the move

- a Premove Calendar (see example, Page 57) so that everyone in the family has an idea of when things will occur or need to be accomplished

Some Unheard-of Moving Tips for Parents

Although most parents have experienced prior moves and have a fairly good idea of the various steps involved in the moving process, it is always helpful to remind yourself that moving with children requires significantly more planning, more energy, and more time than you initially expect. Equally important to remember is that arriving at your new home physically exhausted and emotionally stressed is not the way to enjoy your family's moving adventure. So, before you even get one moment closer to the actual day of your move, here are a few practical, but often unheard of, premove tips for parents:

- Make your own Premove Checklist (see example, Page 55) of things to be done as moving day approaches. Your moving company or any moving handbook will supply you with examples, but the one important thing these guides do not tell you is to be sure to make time for yourself to relax, to have fun, and to share the excitement of moving with your spouse, your roommate, or your friends and neighbors without the kids around.

- Make a personal Premove Calendar to coincide with your Premove Checklist and schedule several dates during the Preparation Stage of your move on which to do something relaxing, fun and energizing for yourself either alone or with your spouse, roommate, friends and neighbors without the kids around.

Practical Moving Tools For Families

- Use a notepad or blank book as a Moving Journal to help keep yourself organized, to record your thoughts, feelings and memories related to the move, and to recall significant events during the course of the moving journey.

- During the Preparation Stage schedule some time for yourself—even as little as fifteen minutes each day—after you've put the kids to bed to relax, unwind, meditate, fantasize, write in your journal, chat with your spouse or roommate, have a glass of wine or a cup of tea, or take a hot bath to renew your own energy level before the next day begins.

- Establish a Message Moving Board (see example, Page 58) complete with markers or pens, slips of note paper, and thumbtacks on which family members can leave messages, write notes or ask questions of one another regarding move-related activities. Be sure to include some fun notes to one another as well.

- Schedule short family meetings, perhaps once a week, to solve problems. offer reassurance, answer questions, or discuss activity schedules, moving tasks, concerns and feelings about the move.

A Premove Checklist for Kids

A handy tool to encourage children's involvement is a simple checklist of tasks each child must accomplish prior to the move. Ask your children for help on what should be included on the lists, have them draw up, decorate and post the lists, and allow them to negotiate changes with you or with siblings.

Keep the checklist items simple, specific and within the ability range of each youngster. Most important, give the kids lots of positive reinforcement for the tasks they complete. A sample Premove Checklist for kids might include:

Moving With Children

- Put all broken toys, torn clothing, and scrap papers in a "trash" box.

- Put all toys that you don't want or clothes that no longer fit in a "charity" box.

- Print your name and our new address on postcards for your friends (Dad will help you with this).

- Return all library books (and pay fines if necessary).

- Plan an autograph party for your friends (Mom will help with this).

- Pass out pre-addressed postcards to your best friends. (Maybe you could do this at the autograph party.)

- Take some pictures of your favorite places in the neighborhood.

- Pack your toy car collection (seashells, jewelry, marbles, etc.) in a small box.

- Pack all of your books (toys, stuffed animals, shoes, sports equipment, etc.) in separate boxes.

- Pack all of your out-of-season clothes in their own box (Dad will help with this).

- Send change of address postcards for your magazines (Mom will help with this).

- Put rubber bands around your baseball cards and pictures.

- Choose a little gift for your teacher or Sunday School instructor. (Mom or Dad will help you shop for it.)

- Put your favorite clothes (teddy bear, toys, blanket, etc.) in a special box so you can find them right after the move.

- Decide which clothes you would like to wear on moving day.

- Put some books (small toys, games, notebook and crayons, snacks, candy, etc.) in your day-pack to take with you in the car (plane, etc.).

- Return any toys, books, sports equipment, records, clothing, video games, etc. you may have borrowed from friends or neighbors.

- Get back any toys, books, sports equipment, etc., etc. you may have loaned to friends or neighbors.

A Premove Checklist for Parents

Probably the very last thing a parent wants to think about before a move is another list! Moving seems to be an endless ordeal of lists of people to call, addresses to change, bills to pay, errands to run, and belongings to pack, but here is one list unconditionally guaranteed to be fun. And it could keep you sane when the ordeal of packing gets you down.

Just sit back, relax, and allow your creative, romantic self to take over for a minute as you think about the things you would like to do before leaving your present neighborhood or community if you had all the time in the world. Your latest list might include:

- Take a long relaxing walk by yourself and be aware of and see things you've never noticed before.

- Go to a movie, alone or with a close friend, in the middle of the day.

- Spend an afternoon at the art museum.

- Get a body massage or a facial after a hard day of packing.

- Meet your best friend downtown for shopping and lunch.

- Get a baby-sitter for the kids and then meet your spouse or roommate for a romantic dinner at your favorite restaurant.

- Set aside some time to call a good friend in another city "just to talk."

- Take a friend to visit that "one place" in town you've always wanted to see but never have.

- Visit your favorite bookstore to pick out the "perfect" first book to read in your new home.

- Attend a concert or play with your closest friends.

- Pack a "Chaos-Survival Kit" (see Chapter 7) for the first few days in your new home.

You may not have time to complete all (or even many) of the items on your fantasy list, but you should remember that taking care of yourself is one way to insure a more enjoyable move for the entire family. When you are feeling overwhelmed and out of energy because of all the moving chores, choose to do at least one item on your premove checklist. Look upon it as a going away gift to yourself.

Practical Moving Tools For Families

A Premove Calendar for Families

Posting a written schedule of important tasks that have to be completed prior to your move serves two valuable family functions. First, it can help assure your family's working together as a team and staying on a reasonable timetable as moving day approaches. Second, it can help reduce everyone's premove tension by bringing a sense of coordination and predictability to the moving process, something particularly important to children, who naturally experience difficulties dealing with change.

For your calendar use a page or two from a commercially printed calendar or have your youngsters put their premove supplies to practical use by having them draw a family calendar on poster board or a large sheet of paper which can then be filled in with important times, dates and activities.

JULY

SUNDAY	MONDAY	TUESDAY	WEDNESDAY	THURSDAY	FRIDAY	SATURDAY
				1	2 FAMILY MEETING	3 START THROWING OUT JUNK!
4 DAD'S GOING AWAY GOLF TOURNAMENT	5	6	7 MOM DINNER WITH BOOK CLUB	8	9 KATHY'S SLEEP-OVER AT JEN'S	10 TODD'S LAST SOCCER GAME AND TEAM PARTY
11 FAMILY TRIP AND LUNCH AT MUSEUM	12 RETURN ALL LIBRARY BOOKS	13 NON-LUNCH WITH MOLLY DOWNTOWN	14 FAMILY MEETING	15	16 DAD'S GOING AWAY LUNCH AT WORK	17 TODD'S SLEEP-OVER AT BART'S
18 TODD AND KATHY'S AUTOGRAPH PARTY	19 MOM'S LAST DAY AT WORK LUNCH	20	21	22 DAD-DINNER WITH PAT, RON AND MIKE	23 KATHY'S GIRL SCOUT PARTY	24 FAMILY DINNER WITH ROB + SHERI
25 GOING AWAY BRUNCH AT CHURCH FAMILY MEETING	26 HEAVY PACKING PACK CHAOS SURVIVAL KIT	27 PACK, PACK, PACK, PACK, PACK, PACK.	28 MOM + DAD DINNER OUT (NO KIDS ALLOWED)	29 PACKERS ARE COMING!!!	30 FINAL PACKING	31 MOVING DAY AT LAST!

57

Moving With Children

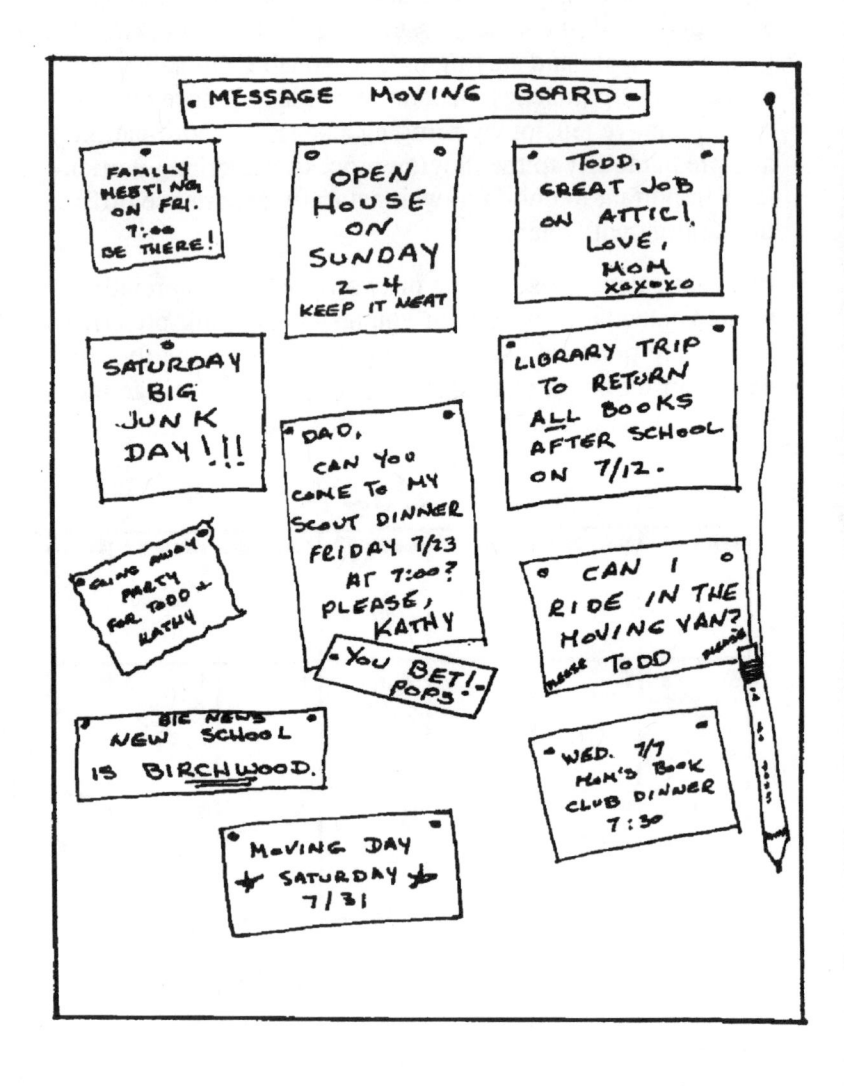

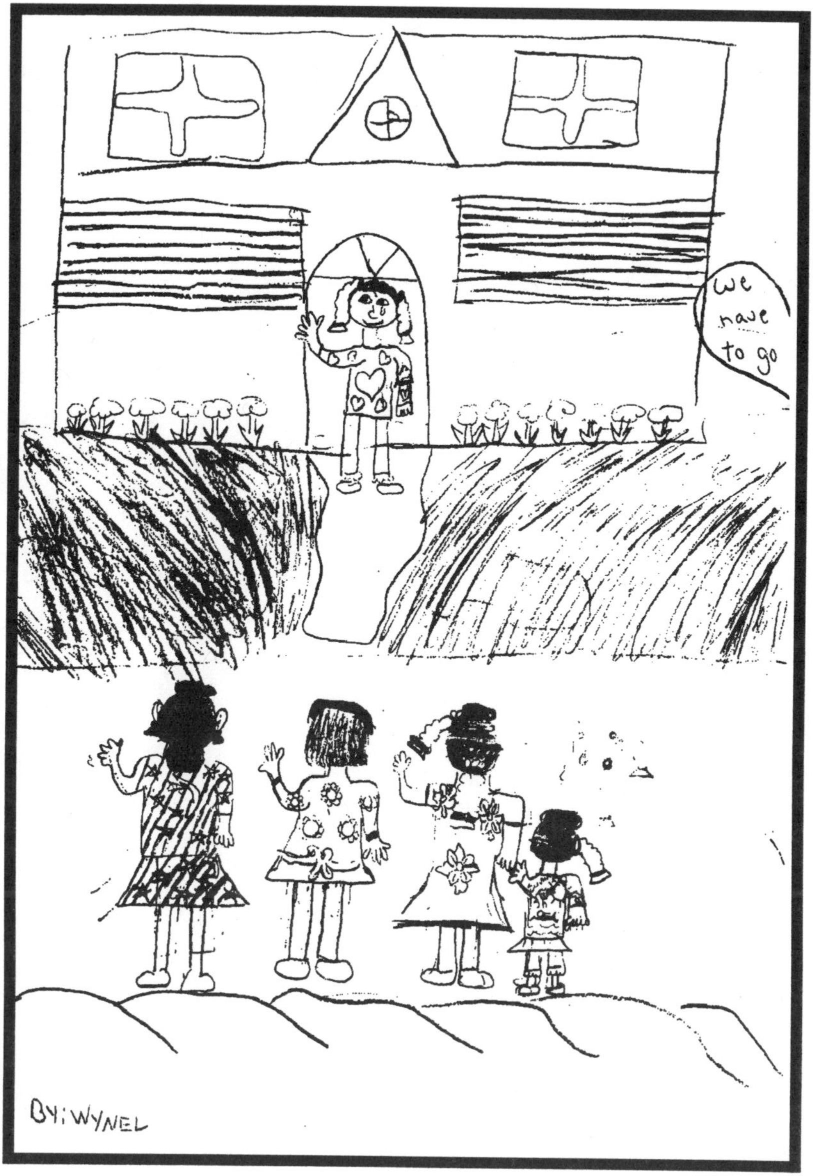
We have to go
BY: WYNEL

CHAPTER 6

Helping Kids Say Goodbye

In his wonderful book *The Way of the Bull,* Leo Buscaglia (9) wrote, " *Though every hello is the beginning of a goodbye, do not lose heart; for every goodbye may also be the beginning of another hello."* As your moving day grows near, bidding farewell to old friends and familiar places can be a difficult task for children and parents alike. Yet saying goodbye to the present is a necessary step we all must take before moving on to whatever the future may hold.

Children's experiences with loss and their abilities to understand or predict a logical sequence of future events are limited. For them moving can be an anxiety-producing experience. Concerns about leaving life-long friends and familiar territory interfere with a child's perception of moving as a potentially enjoyable adventure. Though these fears usually dissipate not long after a move, they can sometimes make the act of moving a traumatic one.

To help your children through this stage of the moving process, try some of the following activities designed to make saying goodbye the first step on a rewarding journey. Be sure, too, to do some creative brainstorming with your kids to come up with your own unique ways of saying goodbye to your old home, friends, and neighborhood.

- Depending on the age of your children, supply each of them with an address book, an autograph book or small photo album to collect addresses. Phone numbers, personal messages, autographs or snapshots of friends and neighbors they might want to keep in touch with.

- Arrange a backyard photo session for your children and their closest friends so they can share photographs with one another before the move.

- Schedule goodbye visits to some of your children's favorite places—a local park, playground or perhaps a restaurant you have all enjoyed.

- Distribute pre-addressed picture postcards to your child's friends or classmates that can be mailed to your new home within a short time after the move.

- Help your children create a neighborhood scrapbook complete with their own drawings or photographs of friends and favorite places.

- Have each child create a list of pleasant memories she or he may want to retain about your present neighborhood or community.

- Ask friends, relatives and neighbors to supply a simple list of questions about your new home and community that children can respond to in writing after you have settled into your new surroundings.

- Arrange with your child's teacher, Sunday School instructor, coach or Scout leader to have a short question-and-answer period in which your child can let classmates or teammates know when and where she or he will be moving. Supply a photograph of your new home for this session if possible.

- Help your child donate a symbolic going-away gift to . her or his school, church or social organization: a small plant, a book for the school library, or an inexpensive piece of equipment the group might need.

- Leave a small memento at your old home that will symbolize your child's life there—planting a flower in the yard, hiding a tiny toy in a secret place, or having the kids write a letter of welcome to the children who will be moving in. A delightful example of just such a moving-away message was recounted to the authors by the parents of a fourteen-year-old girl who, upon moving into her bedroom of the family's new home, discovered a welcoming letter describing all the secret nooks and crannies in the house from the room's prior inhabitant, now a college student. Several months later the girls had an opportunity to meet and became fast friends on the basis of the enjoyment of "their" house.

- Look for frequent opportunities to talk with your kids about their feelings regarding the move and make certain to share yours with them as well.

Keep in mind that your goodbyes are as important as your children's. Although possibly tinged with sadness, your move represents both the completion of a journey and the beginning of a new adventure. Utilize some of the activities on your personal Premove Checklist from Chapter 4 to make your goodbyes both a celebration of the past and a toast to the future with close friends and neighbors. As a special going-away gift to yourself, ask each of your friends for a short list of things they would want to learn or experience were they in your position. Later as you begin to settle in to your new home, refer to these items as special wishes that your friends have bestowed upon you as you begin this new chapter in your life.

Special Goodbyes for Special Moves

By their very nature some moves involve multiple emotional losses that create greater difficulty and demand that more careful attention be paid to the process of saying goodbye for the entire family.

Moves that are necessitated by death of family member can cause such a reaction. A family may have to move for financial reasons because they can no longer afford to maintain their present home after the death of a working parent. They may choose to move for emotional reasons caused by the many memories associated with the deceased in their present home, or the physical nature of the deceased's death may make it advisable that a family move for their emotional well-being.

In such cases it is extremely important for parents to realize that both they and the children are dealing with complex emotional losses. The death of a family member is one of the most stressful events a family can experience, and it requires that the entire family deal with their grief over the loss of a loved one before they can attempt to deal with the other losses usually associated with a move. If at all possible, it is wise to postpone any decision about a move until the family has been able to work through their grief related to the death. If that option is not feasible, parents should pay special attention to the emotional needs of the family and support one another in dealing with the grief, both their own and those of the children.

The trauma of saying goodbye under such conditions can sometimes be eased through a family ritual such as an anonymous contribution of services or goods to an individual or group in memory of the deceased. Such action requires that the family work together to decide what contribution the deceased may have made had she or he lived. Its anonymity lends the ritual a timeless tone that heightens its healing power. Another possible option is a symbolic going-away gift to the deceased such as the planting of a small tree or the burial of farewell messages from the family in the yard of the home being left behind.

Divorce is another significant family change that can force a move and complicate a family's goodbyes. When a divorce causes one or both parents to move, children face not only the sadness at moving but insecurities about the dissolution of the family and concerns for the safety of the noncustodial parent. Regardless of their own relief at being divorced or any antagonism they maintain toward one another, divorcing parents should always try to be aware of the complexity of the emotional losses facing children exposed to both a divorce and a move.

Both parents must strive to assure children that they are not the cause of either the divorce or the move. Despite possible animosity toward one another, parents should try to reassure children about the safety and well-being of the absent parent and to allow children free communication access to the absent parent through visitations, phone calls, letters and tapes. If a child feels secure about the safety of the absent parent and comfortable with the availability of contact with that parent, she or he can proceed more easily with goodbyes related to the move.

The authors found it effective when leading groups for children who had experienced a divorce or death of a parent to have children brainstorm both the advantages and disadvantages of their current situations. Inevitably the change in their family's status had involved a move. Discovering the potential positive opportunities that had occurred because of the move was an eye-opener for the children. Even in the most troubled situations, youngsters could find advantages. This ability to see the possibility hidden in an otherwise difficult situation is one that helps us all travel through life more lightly and with greater dignity.

Some moves present families with less traumatic though equally difficult emotional goodbyes. When long distance moves require that a close relative such as a grandparent or a live-in care provider who has become accepted as an integral part of the family remain behind, special attention should be paid to the entire family's sense of loss. The same is true when older siblings elect to remain at college or at their jobs rather than participate in the family move. In situations such as these, frequent contacts by phone and mail should be maintained among all family members until children appear reassured and comfortable about the safety of those individuals who did not move with the family.

Finally a unique but significant emotional issue arises when a cherished family pet cannot be included in a move. Many overseas relocations force such a decision because of foreign animal-importation laws, and parents should realize that the decision to give up a pet can be as upsetting to the family as the death of a loved one.

If such a loss becomes imminent, all family members should be involved in deciding on a caring home for their pet, and clear-cut agreements should be made regarding its retrieval if the family's relocation is a temporary assignment. Family members should be allowed to deal with their grief about a pet at their own emotional pace just as they would with any loss, and parents should not rush to replace an animal until children express an interest in doing so.

With these, as with all of your goodbyes, be sure to remember that everyone in your family will experience highly individualized feelings about moving and loss that may surface in distinct ways at different times and that may even change from day to day. Don't try to ignore or hurry the process for anyone, including yourself. Saying goodbye is a highly personal but perfectly natural matter you will each have to deal with as a first important step toward making your move a potential "hello" to a positive experience for the entire family.

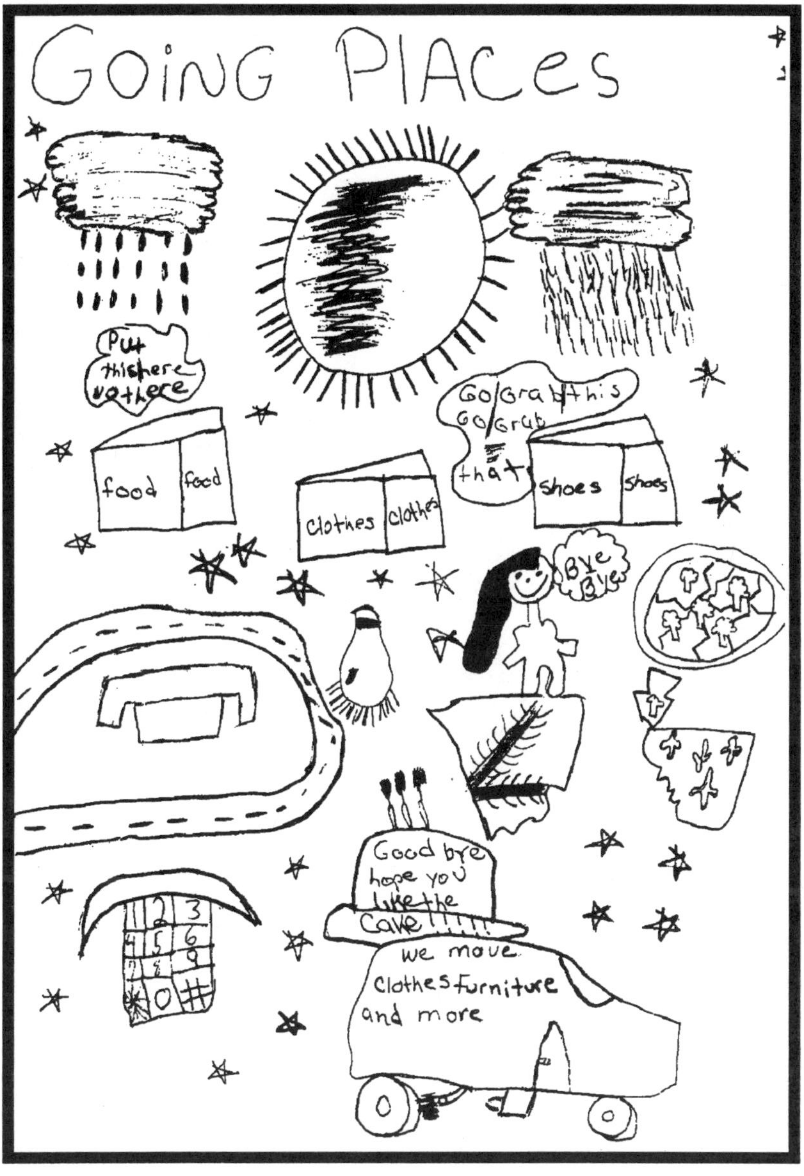
GoinG PlAces
Put thishere notheRe
Go/Grab this
Go/Grab
that
food
food
clothes
clothes
shoes
shoes
Bye Bye
Good bye hope you like the Cave!!!!!
we move
Clothes furniture
and more
1 2 3
4 5 6
7 8 9
* 0 #

CHAPTER 7

Practical Packing For Families

There is one universal rule that governs all family moves: The six to eight weeks you started with in the Preparation Stage will imperceptibly dwindle to what seems like a few scant hours for the Work Stage of your move. During this muscle and sweat period of moving, wrapping, packing, keeping and tossing become the primary family activities, and whatever the reality, it will always feel like there is never enough time for the amount of work that has to be done. It is also during this period that strange things start to happen.

As the time remaining until moving day steadily decreases, stress levels rise. Parents worry more as they attempt to solve a far greater number of problems each day than most people confront in a month. Tempers shorten; parents impulsively snap at children, spouses, pets and anything else that moves of its own accord. Parental expectation levels increase to the extent that adults actually believe that simply making a request for help should result in gracious and instantaneous cooperation from their offspring. It is clearly time for a reality check.

- First, remind yourself that the moving process will inevitably seem more harried and out-of-control the nearer you get to your actual moving day, but that things are not always what they seem. Consider the possibility that you and your family have things under control and that you aren't experiencing anything unusual.

- Second, reassure yourself that, because you and your children have followed through on your Premove Checklists and Calendar, have talked about the move among yourselves, and have taken time to relax and reenergize yourselves, you are on a reasonable schedule and will be ready for moving day when it arrives.

- Finally, remind yourself that any child's typical level of enthusiasm and self-direction in regard to household chores, homework assignments, or any other laborious tasks is usually microscopic. Take a moment to see that you are setting yourself up for undue frustration by believing that your children will work enthusiastically and unsupervised for hours without someone present telling them what to do.

To reduce these Work Stage frustrations before they begin, make certain that the packing tasks you assign your children are reasonable in terms of their ability levels, relatively simple and clearly defined.

- Explain, then demonstrate the tasks and ask questions to insure that the kids know what's expected of them.

- Plan ahead to check in on the kids frequently, to offer repeated encouragement, to lend a helping hand from time to time, and to reinforce them often for small bits of progress.

- Be sure to make tasks more enjoyable by periodically alternating jobs, sometimes working as a group or trading partners, playing word games, telling jokes or singing together as you work, and building in small rewards for the completion of specific tasks.

Practical Packing Supplies for Kids

One way to heighten your kids' enthusiasm for cooperation is to appoint them "honorary movers" with their own set of moving supplies and "official moving caps" which can only be worn when they are actively involved in packing and moving chores. Caps with your children's names on them not only prevent arguments about who's wearing the right cap but later become handy getting-acquainted tools when your kids set out to meet other children in your new neighborhood.

A practical and interest-arousing set of individualized packing supplies for kids might include:

- lots of trash bags (and then a few more)

- several clean, sturdy boxes that can easily be written on with markers or crayons

- plenty of newspapers to wrap breakable items

- a set of colored pens, crayons or washable markers, preferably in different colors for each child, for marking boxes that have been packed

- a roll of masking or packing tape to seal boxes

- a set of packing labels or colorful stickers, preferably in different colors or styles for each youngster, for easy identification once the boxes get moved

- pre-marked boxes or bags for toys or clothing to be given to charity and another set for trash to be thrown out

- a number of smaller boxes or plastic bags for small toys, collections, marbles, jewelry, etc. along with a supply of rubber bands to secure them

- specially marked boxes for out-of-season clothing and equipment

- another set of pre-labeled boxes for clothing and items that will be used immediately following the move

- at least one distinctively marked box for favorite toys, stuffed animals, blankets, books, nightlights or whatever items each child "absolutely can't live without" immediately following the move

- any special packing materials necessary for the moving of pets or plants

- at least one large box for all the last minute "I forgots."

- a daypack for cherished items, such as books, small toys, a notebook, pencils or crayons, games, snacks, candy that each child will carry during the actual move

A Chaos-Survival Kit for Parents

Just prior to moving day, after you've packed your furniture, belongings, children's belongings, pets' belongings, plants, and any other items you haven't been able to sell, donate, give away, lose or forget, be sure to take an hour or so to pack a personal survival kit containing your favorite "calming the chaos" treats to celebrate with right after the kids are put to bed on the first night in your new home. Take your Chaos-Survival Kit with you in the car, carry it with you on the plane, and mark it well so it doesn't get lost in the shuffle. It is your reward for a job well done and a signal that it is time to relax, celebrate, and begin enjoying your new home.

Here are a few examples of the supplies you might want to include for yourself:

- a portable coffee maker, freshly-ground coffee (or tea), filters, sugar packets, creamer, spoons, and a few of your favorite mugs

- a bottle of champagne, wine, sparkling water, fruit juice, beer, soda pop—whatever you (and your roommate or spouse) use to toast a moment of celebration

- a packet of your favorite snacks—cookies, crackers, candies, pretzels, fruit...

- candles for a candlelight (take-out) dinner on the dining room floor, a picnic in the yard, or to set a relaxing mood in the bath or bedroom

- your favorite bath gel, soap, shampoo, conditioner, and other assorted toiletries to allow you to clean up or perhaps just soak in the tub and relax after a tiring moving day

- some clean, comfortable clothes or nightwear to slip into that will signal that the work of moving day is finished

- a portable radio or tape player and some calming or energizing music

- that "perfect" moving day book you bought yourself earlier as a going-away gift

- your Moving Journal to record the thoughts, feelings, experiences, and memories—both the ups and downs—of your moving day

- several written reminders to yourself (and your spouse or roommate) to take some uninterrupted time to relax and enjoy the end of a hectic day

If you engage in any activities like running that require special equipment or clothing, pack your gear separately and label it clearly or hand-carry it, if necessary. Several years ago, one of the authors carefully packed his trout-fishing gear in a carton marked "Master Bedroom" so that he could find it easily and enjoy a few hours of quiet relaxation during the week following his family's move. Remember, exercise is a great way to reduce stress and renew energy to help you through the initial stages of the post-move period in your new home.

When Moving Day Finally Arrives

For many families moving day can seem like a hectic combination of Christmas Eve, the last day of school before summer vacation, and the first day of heavy spring cleaning. It's a day of hard work, anticipation and excitement, uncertainty about what might lie ahead, and a sense of sadness at saying goodbye to your old home and neighborhood. And young children are especially vulnerable to the many feelings that may arise on moving day.

Most children quickly get caught up in the spirit of the day, wanting to help with packing and loading one moment but possibly feeling confused and uncertain the next. They may become tearful and sad about leaving a neighbor friend, fret about a treasured toy or pet being left behind, worry about what their new home will be like, or simply feel overwhelmed with the frantic activity.

With some advanced planning and a few simple strategies however, you can reassure your youngsters and help them enjoy the adventure of this special day.

- The best way to approach moving day is with a simple ounce of prevention. On the night before your move make sure that all of you get a good night's sleep so that you are refreshed and rested when the physical labor actually begins.

- On moving day arrange to have a friend, a neighbor or a relative look out for the kids. Keep them close by so they can see what's going on but out from under the movers' feet.

- Check in with them regularly to answer questions, offer emotional support, and give them plenty of reassurance and encouragement.

- In packing, use specially marked boxes so the kids' items are easily distinguishable from others in the family. When moving them, try to position the children's things so they can be unloaded all at one time and early in the move.

- If the children are old enough, assign them simple, specific tasks so they can feel actively involved, perhaps allowing them to load small furnishings or cartons from their rooms so they can feel assured that their most important possessions won't be forgotten.

- Have each child set aside a daypack with her or his most cherished items, a favorite book or teddy bear, pajamas, blanket, toothbrush and nightlight and any other "absolute necessities" they can personally carry with them during the move.

- Take special care to assure youngsters that the family pets are safe and cared for during the move.

- If you are driving a considerable distance, pack a cooler with fruit, juice, soda pop and favorite snacks and sandwiches to keep hunger from making kids or parents irritable.

- Take along a supply of car games, books, toys, pillows, blankets and perhaps a personal portable stereo with your children's favorite music or story tapes to keep them occupied.

When you arrive at your new home, have the movers set up the furniture in your children's rooms first to help establish a sense of familiarity and comfort for them. The kids can then keep busy unpacking and putting away their toys and clothing, and it will give them a place to play and later to nap as the rest of your family belongings are unloaded.

With the kids finally tucked into bed, the hard work of moving day may not be over yet. But with some simple planning for your children, you can all breathe a bit easier and make moving day an enjoyable introduction to your family's new home.

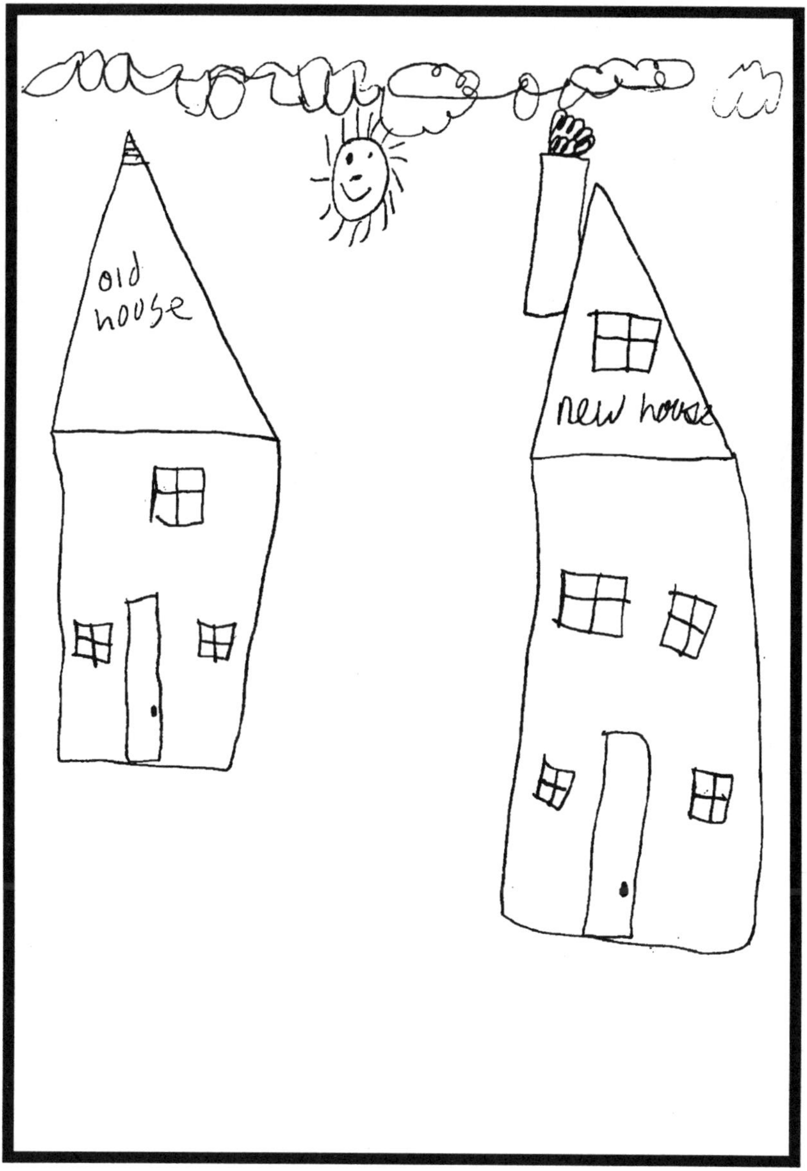
old house
new house

CHAPTER 8

Well, We're Here. Now What?

The third and final step of your move, the Settling-in Stage, begins the moment you, your kids, pets, plants, furniture, cartons, and assorted family belongings arrive safely on the doorstep of your new house, apartment, condominium, cabin or castle. It is complete only when you all stop referring to your "new house" and start perceiving it as "our house" or better yet "our home."

The Settling-in Stage of a move requires two different kinds of work from families, one physical, the other social and emotional. The physical labor at this point is rather obvious. A move is only half completed when you arrive at your new home. Then comes the labor of unloading, unpacking, sorting, setting up and arranging, then rearranging furniture, cleaning, putting away, decorating, and simply finding your way around your new house.

The social and emotional work of this stage includes becoming comfortable in the house, finding your way around the neighborhood and community, discovering shops, services, and places of interest that are important to your family's needs, meeting new neighbors, dealing with the sadness of saying goodbye, becoming familiar with new jobs and schools, making new friends, and discovering new favorite places that will ultimately make your new house a real home.

Naturally the vastly different aspects of the physical and emotional jobs that face you during the Settling-in Stage require different approaches as well as a unique set of tools designed for each task. The good news is that you're more than halfway there, and many of the strategies and suggestions you've already tried prior to the move will work just as well now with only a few modifications and a little bit of imagination, creativity and sense of adventure from you and your family.

Moving-in Supplies for Kids

Imagine for a second pulling up in front of your new home. You are eager to get your belongings unloaded and unpacked, knowing that once this step is accomplished you will be able to take some time to relax, and you are still expecting (though hopefully more realistically now) some help and cooperation from the kids.

Instead what typically occurs is that the kids jump out of the car before it has come to a complete stop. They zoom into the house to begin exploring the basement, bedrooms, backyard, attic, crawlspace, and garage, or worse they commence arguing about who got the "better" room.

At this point it would probably be best to let out a giant sigh, take some satisfaction in knowing that this is exactly what you expected, and give yourself a pat on the back for being fully prepared for these events. Allow the kids their opportunities for exploration; moving day is the beginning of new discoveries for all of you. Remind yourself that the way you gained cooperation from them prior to the move was by assigning them short, specific tasks, making jobs fun, checking in on them frequently, offering repeated encouragement, lending them a helping hand from time to time, and reinforcing them for small bits of progress. You can then rekindle their spirit of cooperation at least long enough to get unpacked by offering each of them an individualized set of moving-in supplies which might include:

- more trash bags

- a surprise package of your child's favorite snacks and treats

- a Post-Move Checklist (see example, Page 83) of simple tasks you would like each child to accomplish immediately following the move

- a Post-Move Calendar (see example, Page 85) so that everyone in the family has an idea what things need to be accomplished and when they will occur

- masking tape, thumb tacks or picture hangers to be used for hanging posters, photographs, pennants or models

- several clean, empty boxes to store toys, clothing, and sports equipment that gets unpacked but won't be used or put away immediately

- clothes hangers and hooks that can be mounted if none are available

- a map of the neighborhood large enough to draw in locations of important places such as the school, playground, park, library once you begin to explore your new surroundings

- a packet of photographs and information (which can be obtained from the Chamber of Commerce, tourism bureau or your moving company in advance) about places of interest for kids and families in your new community

- a "new neighborhood" scrapbook to be filled in as you and your children begin to explore your new surroundings

- a few more rolls of film so that your children can take photos of the new neighborhood for their scrapbooks or to send to friends

- a Neighborhood Discovery Board (Chapter 9)

- a small amount of money for your child to buy a special "moving-in gift" for her or his room or a symbolic "moving in surprise" for your child based on your knowledge of her or his interests. A personalized tee-shirt, for example, can double as both a "moving-in gift" for your youngster as well as a handy means of letting kids in the neighborhood know what your child's name is.

Some Unheard-of Unpacking Tips for Parents

Moving day is an exhausting one both emotionally and physically with still much more to do, but now that you've arrived safely in your new home, there is no rule that states you can't take some time to relax and start enjoying your new abode before everything is unpacked and put away. As a matter of fact, now might be the very best time for you and your spouse or roommate to celebrate your successful relocation by trying some of these unheard-of unpacking tips for parents.

- After you or the movers have arranged the furniture in Your children's rooms, make your bedroom the next priority on the list so that you can prepare the bed with some fresh, perhaps newly-purchased, linens to be ready for your weary bodies at the end of the day.

- Buy a gigantic bouquet of freshly cut flowers and place them in a vase for everyone to see as a color treat among the still unpacked cartons.

- Order some good take-out food and desserts for a no cleanup dinner on the dining room floor or a picnic in the backyard.

Well, We're Here. Now What?

- Break out your "Chaos-Survival Kit" and then take a long, hot bath or shower to get rid of the grime of the day, slip into some fresh, comfortable clothes, make a pot of wonderful coffee or hot tea, or share a toast with your spouse or roommate.

- Set up your portable stereo or radio and find some music you all enjoy; or later after the kids are asleep, ask your spouse or roommate to dance to "your" song in the midst of all the unpacked cartons.

- Surprise your spouse or roommate with a thoughtful but totally impractical (romantic) "moving-in" gift, or give one to yourself.

- Before settling in for the night, give each other a back rub or a foot massage to get rid of some of the muscle aches after a long day of hard work.

- Curl up with that "perfect" moving day book and a glass of wine or cup of tea, or simply slip into bed and get a great night's sleep in your new home.

* * * * *

A Post-move Checklist for Families

The first few weeks immediately after move can be somewhat harried for kids and parents alike, but using a checklist of family activities similar to your children's premove checklist can make life more predictable, reduce anxiety, and help everyone feel more productive and comfortable during the Settling-in Stage of your move.

Keep the list simple, specific, and related to your family's interests and special needs. Above all, make sure you all work together on it as a team. Here are just a few examples of things you may want to include:

Moving With Children

- Throw out all empty boxes, trash, and packing materials we are finished with, and relax a little.

- Take a short walk or bike ride around the neighborhood at least once a day.

- Start meeting our new neighbors. Start working on our Neighborhood Map and our Neighborhood Discovery Board.

- Meet the mailman.

- Mail postcards to friends in our old neighborhood.

- Find out where the school, post office, library and shopping mall are.

- Get new library cards.

- Call the neighborhood "welcome service."

- Find out where the neighborhood kids hang out.

- Find out where the church is and meet the minister.

- Register Todd and Kathy for school.

- Get a city bus schedule.

- Find out where the park and the recreation center are.

- Find a movie theater, a hobby shop, toy store and video rental.

- Go on a sightseeing trip.

- Have our own moving-in celebration!

Well, We're Here. Now What?

A Post-Move Calendar for Families

Immediately following your move, the hectic planning and scheduling you experienced prior to getting to this point will no longer weigh as heavily upon your family. Instead, a new timetable governed by school registrations, soccer schedules, music lessons, and a host of necessary settling-in errands will take its place.

An extremely useful tool to insure that your settling-in period is a smooth and enjoyable one is a post-move calendar with a focus on activities that help you feel comfortable in your new neighborhood, provide information about the community, and allow you some family relaxation before you all settle back into a regular daily routine.

August

Sunday	Monday	Tuesday	Wednesday	Thursday	Friday	Saturday
1 HEAVY UNPACKING, HEAVY RESTING, NEIGHBORHOOD WALK	2 FAMILY MEETING — NEIGHBORHOOD WALK	3	4 GRAB BAG EXPLORER	5 VISIT MALL	6 GRAB BAG EXPLORER	7 FIND A GREAT PIZZA!
8 VISIT DOWNTOWN LUNCH OUT	9 DAD STARTS NEW JOB	10	11 GRAB BAG EXPLORER	12	13 FAMILY MEETING	14 DINNER OUT AND MOVIE
15 PICNIC IN CITY PARK	16 REGISTER TODD AND KATHY FOR SCHOOL	17 LET MOM RELAX	18 MOM STARTS WORK, KIDS COOK DINNER	19	20 GRAB BAG EXPLORER + ICE CREAM	21 FIND LIBRARY, POST OFFICE, BOOKSTORE
22 GO TO A BALL GAME	23 SIGN UP FOR SOCCER	24	25 GRAB BAG EXPLORER — SCHOOL SHOPPING	26	27 MOM AND DAD DINNER ALONE	28 NEW NEIGHBOR PICNIC AT SMITHS
29 GET READY FOR TOMORROW →	30 SCHOOL STARTS Boo!	31				

Moving With Children

TARGET Outlet
Western
Bank
Western
GAS
Rent
a
Van
333-3333
1059
welcome

CHAPTER 9

Exploring Your New Neighborhood

Often overlooked in the hubbub of moving is the fact that moving day, that eagerly awaited yet almost dreaded date on your calendar, brings everyone in the family face-to-face with those mixed emotions that you have all handled so well up to this point. Fantasy has become reality and in your spare moments between opening another carton and putting away the next dish, you may begin to recognize renewed doubts and anxieties. At this point it is perfectly natural to experience questions about whether you will enjoy your new home, school or job, sadness about leaving old friends, neighbors or business colleagues, and concerns about meeting new people and establishing new relationships, all mixed with the anticipation of enjoyment and adventure.

Even before the sun has set on the first day in your new home, your children's excitement about moving will give way to curiosity about your new surroundings. Despite the work still to be done in terms of unpacking and settling in, kids' attentions will naturally turn to issues most important to them. Who lives in this neighborhood? Do any other kids live around here? Are they friendly? Where's the school? And is there a hobby shop, a playground, a skating rink, a record store, or a fast food restaurant nearby?

As we discussed earlier, parents' tasks at this point include trying to be aware of and acknowledging how family members might be feeling, answering questions, reassuring and comforting, sharing their own feelings openly, keeping family stress to a minimum, and acting as role models for openness, curiosity and excitement regarding the move. Finally, parents should realize that their primary task is to help kids develop a sense of comfort and identity with their new community, for with these feelings will come the security and confidence children need to allow them to explore their surroundings and establish new relationships on their own.

To aid in this task, here is a list of specific suggestions to help you begin to explore your new neighborhood and community.

- If you are moving to another location within your present community, take a series of family exploration trips during the month prior to the move to give your children an opportunity to become familiar with the new neighborhood.

- If you are moving into a home previously occupied by a family with children, ask if they would be willing to leave the names, ages and addresses of nearby children or perhaps a list of favorite play areas, neighborhood activities, or specialty stores to give your children a child's perspective of the neighborhood.

- Take your children along on necessary moving-day errands to the hardware store, the grocery or the drug store as a way of introducing them to the new neighborhood and having them feel involved in the move.

- Take short family walks as a way of unwinding from the physical rigors of the move and to make initial explorations of your new surroundings. This is also a great way to meet new neighbors and potential playmates for your children.

- When the dust from the move has settled a bit, have the kids help draw a neighborhood map with locations of important places such as the school, playground, commu-

Exploring Your New Neighborhood

nity center, shopping area, and toy store, so they can feel more confident about finding their way around.

- Set specific goals for exploring your new community like: visiting the recreation center, getting library cards, meeting the mail carrier, touring the local museum, or visiting the town center.

- Schedule discovery days for locating important shops, services and places of interest to your family and make exploring more enjoyable by using a Neighborhood Discovery Board (see example, Page 100) or playing Grab Bag Explorers (see example, Page 96).

- Investigate local groups and activities that your family may have been involved with in your former community—churches, Scouts, sports, or social, ethnic and cultural organizations.

- Look into family and kids only activities offered through children's and historical museums, the zoo, recreation centers, schools, libraries, toy and hobby shops, and local bookstores. Most communities have at least one free newspaper containing listings and schedules for such activities.

- Discover the unique cultural aspects of your new community by participating in community-wide celebrations and festivals or even taking a guided tour of major points of interest.

- When you are feeling more settled, invite immediate neighbors, especially those with children, for a backyard lunch or cookout so that you can get to know each other in a relaxed, informal atmosphere.

- If neighborhood children live nearby, arrange to have them show you and your children the routes they usually follow when walking to school, the playground, the pool, or the recreation center.

- ♦ Once you have established a relationship with a dependable neighborhood baby-sitter, plan an afternoon visit and have the sitter bring along another child that he or she sits for of the same age as your child.

- ♦ Create a neighborhood scrapbook with photos or the kids' drawings of new neighbors, playmates and local sights both as a memento of your move and to show to old friends who visit your new home.

Tools for Exploring Your Neighborhood

There are certainly no specific rules for becoming acquainted with your new surroundings after moving day. How soon you begin, how long you take, and what specific places you choose to explore in your new community are strictly a matter of individual energy, preference and need that your family will decide on at its own pace.

Here, however, are some potential tools for exploring in an enjoyable fashion. As you read through them, remember that they are simply ideas to stimulate you and your children into creating imaginative strategies of your own for investigating your new locale.

The Neighborhood Discovery Board

In Chapter 4 we suggested that prior to your move you establish a Message Moving Board complete with markers, pens, slips of note paper, and thumbtacks. On your board family members can leave messages, write notes, or ask questions of one another. You can now utilize this same technique for a Neighborhood Discovery Board (see example, Page 100) where all family members can jot down important questions, share information or announce discoveries about your new home, neighborhood and community. Just a few examples might include:

Exploring Your New Neighborhood

- Does anybody know where the school is yet?—Todd

- We'll find out on Monday when we register.—Dad

- Has anyone seen my tennis shoes?—Kathy

- They got mixed up with my running clothes.—Mom

- Does anyone know who the kid across the street is?—Todd

- His name's Jamie. He's 10, and his sister Julie is 12. They both seem pretty nice.—Kathy

- I met his mom, and she says you'll be in the same class he is.—Mom

- Is there a record store around here?—Kathy

- We'll have to find out this weekend after your rooms are picked up. And I need to find a good dry cleaners.—Mom

- How about a hobby shop?—Todd

- This weekend, after the rooms are picked up.—Mom

- How about a great pizza????—Dad

- The neighbor mentioned a place called "The Saucy Noodle," but you have to pick your room up first!—Mom

- Yeah, Dad, pick your room up first!—Todd

- When is trash day?—Dad

- I think it's Friday.— Mom

- You know what that means, Todd.—Dad

- Yuck!!!—Todd

- How about if we visit the recreation center on Sunday? I'll even buy ice cream for everyone.—Dad

- I'll go!—Todd

- Me too!!—Kathy

- Me three!!! But I want a sundae!!!—Mom

A Neighborhood Map

Another easy and enjoyable method for helping all of you become more familiar with the immediate neighborhood is to use a large sheet of poster board or butcher paper and some colorful markers with which to draw a map of the various streets in the vicinity surrounding your new home. Then as you discover the locations of shops, schools, the homes of various neighbor children, and other places of interest to your family, you can begin to enter them on your Neighborhood Map (see example, Page 101).

The Neighborhood Yellow Pages

Along with your Neighborhood Map, another practical tool for becoming familiarized and comfortable in your new community is a pad, notebook or loose-leaf binder near the phone with an attached pen or pencil to list addresses and phone numbers of nearby neighbors, service people, and potential baby-sitters as well as other entries such as names and locations of various shops and services, restaurants (along with critical comments), movie theaters, bus schedules, important dates to keep in mind, and any other information that might be of interest or use to your family. Here are just a few examples:

- Neighbors: Bill and Sheila Smith—White house across the street. Jamie (10) is in Todd's grade. Julie is 12. They both like to play soccer.

- Birchwood Elementary School: Corner of 3rd and Birch. School registration next Monday. Mrs. Young is the principal.

- Bijou Theater: 1st and Madison, Children's matinee at 11:00 on Saturdays, Dollar movie nights on Wednesday.

- The Saucy Noodle Restaurant: Bill Smith recommends the pizza! Let's try it this weekend.

- Library: 316 Oak Street. Kids' story hour every Friday at 1:00 until school starts.

- Mr. Jackson: Handyman, 333-1700.

- Trash pick-up: Friday mornings about 8:30 A.M.

- Community Picnic: Labor Day weekend at City Hall Park.

- Fillmore Church: 8th and Logan, Newcomers' breakfast after services on Sunday. Reverend Murphy.

- Bus #32 goes all the way downtown from 1st and Grape every half hour every day but Sunday, 75 cents.

Grab Bag Explorers

If your family is the type of group that enjoys playing games, having fun together, and is comfortable with minimum amounts of planning or structure, you can turn the exploration of your new community into a family game like Grab Bag Explorers.

Moving With Children

Start by holding a short family meeting at which everyone brainstorms ideas of places they would like to discover or explore in your new neighborhood. Jot each of these ideas on slips of paper and dump them into a container. Needless to say, there should be one or two small boxes left over from the move lying around that will work just fine for this purpose.

Then, on designated discovery days, perhaps on weekends or a couple evenings during the week after chores are completed, take turns pulling a few discovery goals from your grab bag and set out to explore them. If someone in the family has already uncovered the location of your discovery destination, that person can then act as your tour guide on that particular day as well as enter the location on the Neighborhood Map.

This strategy allows all family members to feel involved in the discovery process and lends an air of mystery and surprise to your explorations. Be as imaginative as you wish in brainstorming your explorations and make sure your list includes plenty of places that each of you would enjoy discovering. A sample Grab Bag Explorers List might include:

a movie theater	the shopping mall
a hobby shop	a sporting goods store
the nearest church	Todd and Kathy's school
the recreation center	a city park
the swimming pool	the art museum
a great coffee shop	a video arcade
a bowling alley	a roller rink
a pet shop	the baseball field
Mom's office	a record shop
a video rental store	a great restaurant for pizza

Exploring Your New Neighborhood

good Chinese takeout	a nice outdoor cafe
an ice cream store	a bike trail
a volleyball court	a playground with lots of kids
an outdoor market	a good department store
the historical museum	a neat place for a picnic
a place to go fishing	a quiet place for lunch
a comfortable hair salon	the public library
the post office	Dad's office
a soccer field	the community college
a hardware store	a good hamburger place
a card and gift shop	an art supply store
a toy store	tennis courts
a golf course	a great bookstore

Let Your Fingers Do the Exploring

For many families perhaps one of the easiest and most effective tools for exploring a new community is also the most accessible—the advertising section of your local telephone directory.

Simply select various sections of the Yellow Pages that are of most interest to you and your children, e.g. Amusements, Libraries, Sports, Theaters, Restaurants, Museums, and look through them together to decide which your family might want to investigate. An added bonus to this simple method is that most city directories include street guides, city maps, information about mass transit, civic and cultural events, places of community and historic interest, and even discount coupons for local merchants and attractions.

Your real estate agent can be another valuable resource in exploring your community. Most realtors provide welcome packets that highlight important and useful information about your new community and neighborhood. Some realtors whom we've interviewed even provide names, ages and fees of nearby baby-sitters and specialized neighborhood directories listing the names of families on each block according to numerical address sequence to make it easier to discover who you new neighbors are.

Here are also a few ideas for adult explorers to investigate without the kids:

- If you exercise, find a health club, a community center with a gymnasium, basketball court, pool, or exercise classes, a running trail, a bike path, or the nearest tennis courts. It's important to keep up your workouts, especially during the stressful times immediately following your move.

- Make a point of discovering a quiet breakfast spot (not a "family" restaurant), a great coffee shop, or an outdoor cafe where you can spend some time alone pretending that you are not a parent for a little while. Make it your oasis of calm away from home where you can write in your journal, people-watch, or simply sit and relax.

- Visit the local library, the art museum, or a bookstore. They are often good sources of information about what may be happening culturally in your new community, and more important, they are usually quiet and relaxing. Many libraries and museums also offer activities for children that would allow you at least an hour a week to read or relax on your own.

- Buy a local bike trail map and take walks or bike rides through different neighborhoods to familiarize yourself with your new surroundings.

- If you live close enough to your former home to continue utilizing your regular baby-sitter until you find a new one, arrange a quiet evening out with your spouse or roommate on a regular basis to check out new restaurants, go to the movies, or just discover places you might enjoy together.

- Consult the entertainment or cultural sections of the newspaper or look for local weekly papers (usually free at libraries, museums and bookstores) that describe community events, concerts, art openings, classes, lectures and sports events, and choose a different activity to try each week.

Above all, keep in mind that regardless of how busy you are during and immediately after moving day, it is important to take the little extra time it requires to plan activities for yourself and your family that will help you get acquainted with your new community and make your move a satisfying family adventure that you can all enjoy.

Moving With Children

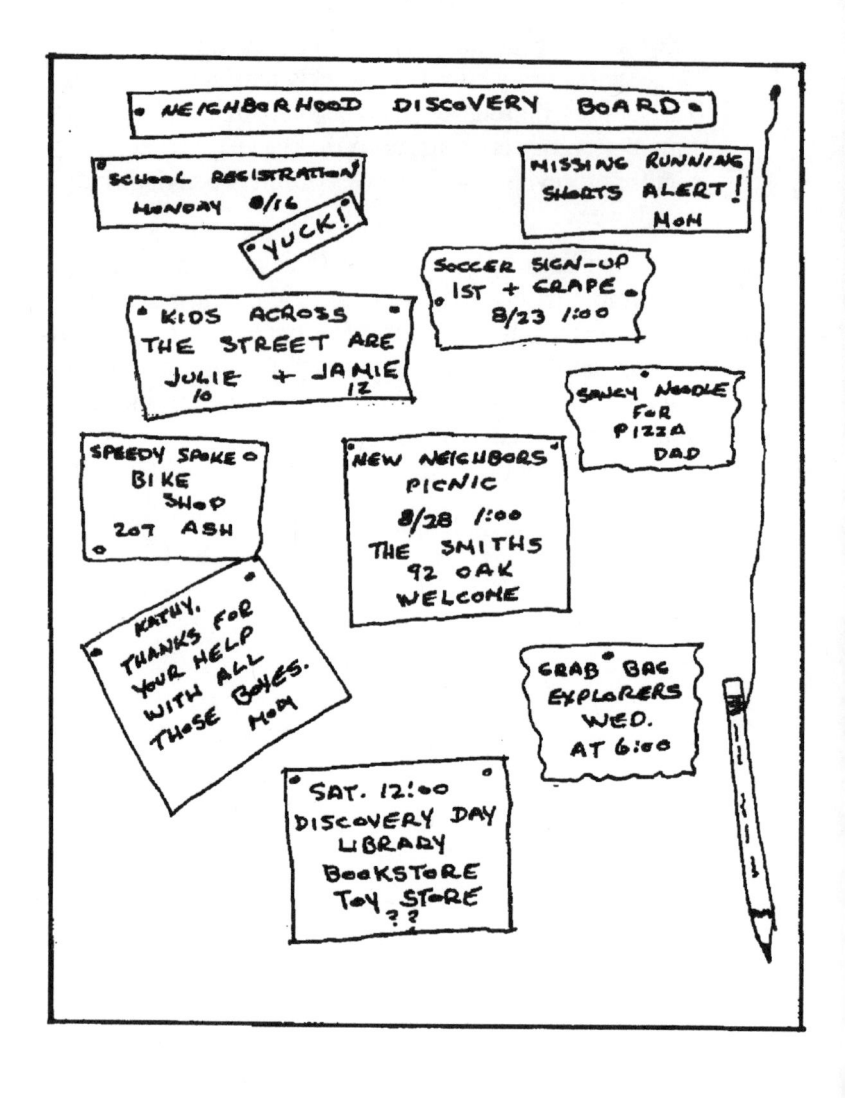

Exploring Your New Neighborhood

Neighborhood Map

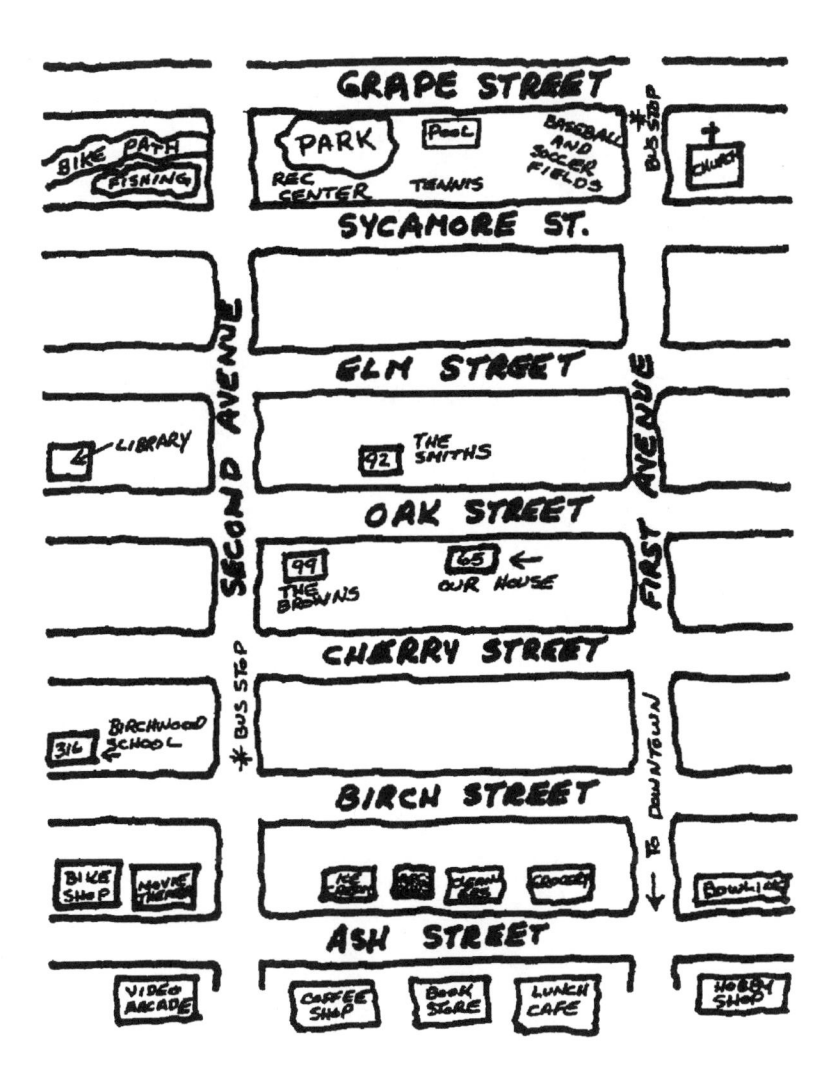

Moving With Children

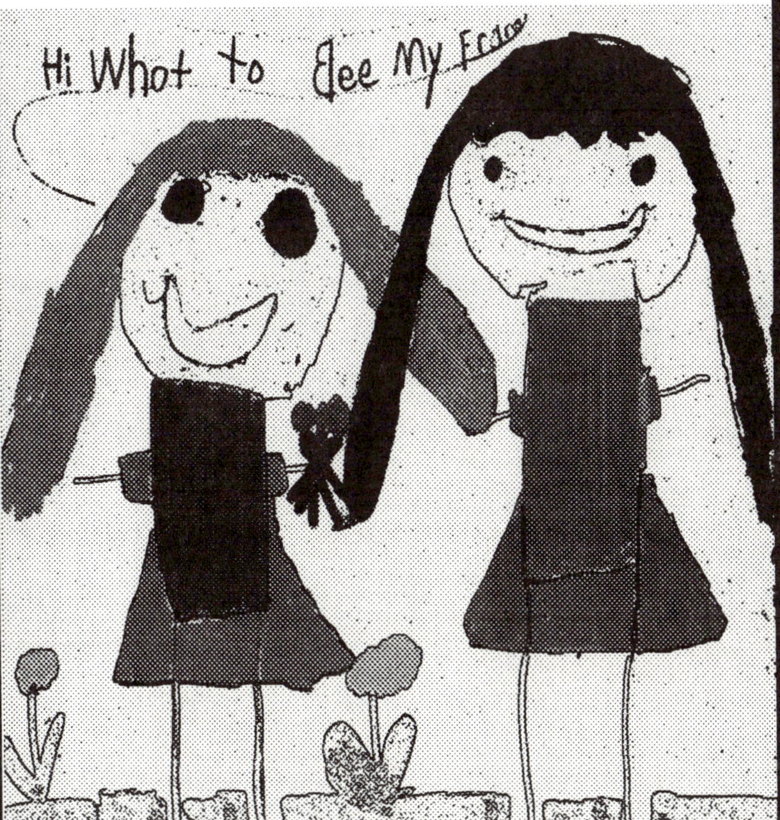
Hi Whot to Elee My

CHAPTER 10

Making Friends In A New School And Neighborhood

Not long after the moving van has rolled away and the empty cartons have been stacked on the back porch, the concerns of almost every child facing a move to an unfamiliar neighborhood or a new school will turn to the questions: "Will there be any other kids there my age?" "Will the kids in my class be nice?" "Will they like me?" "What if they're mean?" and "Will I have any friends?"

At about the same time, parents will begin unpacking their concerns and sometimes struggling with their own fears and anxieties about their youngsters' abilities to adjust to the move. The questions parents seem to ask most frequently are: "How will the move affect my children?" "Will my kids be able to adapt to the new school or neighborhood?" "Will they be happy there?" and "Will they get along with the other children and make new friends?" If parents sense that their youngsters are having difficulty adjusting to the new setting or are not establishing friendships, their first question is, "What can I do to help?"

For parents with such concerns, it is important to realize first that a family move is a major life change and that adjusting to it will take some time. Some families may take six months to a year and a half to become fully settled. Also important to remember is that you cannot fashion your children's adjustment or manufacture their happiness with your new surroundings any more than you can go out and create new friendships for them.

What you can do to help is to reassure your kids about their abilities to explore and adjust on their own. Simply being there when they feel the need to talk will strengthen their sense of comfort and identity with your new home and community and allow them to try different strategies that will eventually result in new friendships.

Listen to and accept your child's feelings about the move without being critical, defensive, or projecting your feelings onto your youngster. Ask clarifying questions when your child does talk about her or his attempts to meet other children. Offer reassurance and simple, specific suggestions, and share some of your own experiences in trying to meet people and make new friends.

Finally, don't take it personally if your child doesn't accept or act upon your advice immediately. Making friends is a highly individualized process and what feels comfortable and successful to one person may not seem even remotely acceptable to another. Furthermore, most children are convinced that adults, even loving parents, are incapable of understanding how kids feel. They are certain that Mom and Dad have never experienced anything quite like these present feelings of being the new kid on the block.

With this in mind, we asked our "kid experts" the question, "If you were new to a school or a neighborhood and didn't know any other kids, what things do you think you could do to meet new people and make friends?" Sharing some of these ideas with your kids may help them realize that they aren't alone in their present feelings and that there are some practical strategies they can use to overcome the getting acquainted dilemma.

Making Friends In A New School And Neighborhood

Tips From Kids to Kids About Making Friends

- It's hard for other kids to get to know you if you never talk to them. So just start talking. You'll make friends soon.

- Be outgoing and be yourself like you were with your old friends. Pretend you're in your old school and that people want to meet you.

- Talk to the kids who sit around you in school and at the bus stop or on the school bus, on the playground before school starts, at recess, or when you're walking home from school.

- Just start by saying "Hi." Tell them you're new and where you're from. Introduce yourself and ask their names, or ask some questions about them like, "How long have you gone to this school?" Or compliment them like, "That's a neat shirt." Say something that makes them feel good about themselves.

- Be nice to everybody, but see if you can find kids who are interested in the same things you are. Look around the class and try to find kids who are a little bit like you. If you see someone who looks friendly, ask him if you could sit with him at lunch or hang around with him on the playground at recess.

- Find out if there are any other new kids that don't have many friends so that you can make friends together. If you see a kid who's all alone, go up and talk to him and ask him to play.

- Ask kids to tell you about the school and the school rules or your teachers. Or ask them to show you around the school, like where the playground and the gym and the lunch room are.

- Act interested in what other kids are doing. Try to fit in. Go with the flow and do what the other kids do. Ask if you can join in their games or work on a school project with them.

- Make yourself recognizable. Raise your hand and answer questions in class. Try to make yourself part of the class. Cooperate with other kids or try to help them with school subjects.

- Be nice to kids and try to treat them like you want to be treated. Be helpful and considerate. Offer to help if a person has a problem or gets hurt. Help someone pick something up if she or he's dropped it, do someone a favor like loaning a pencil or some paper, or share a snack.

- Join in school activities like the Cub Scouts, the soccer team, or a school club. Go to school dances and parties, or join a club at church.

- At home spend a lot of time outside until you see some kids you can meet. Get around the neighborhood a lot—walk your dog or ride your bike, and if you see someone, just say "Hi." Sometimes if you play outside by yourself, kids will come over and ask you to play.

- When you meet your neighbors, ask them if they have kids. Look for kids your age and try to find out where they live. And if you meet some kids, ask them if they would show you around the neighborhood and introduce you to their other friends.

- Visit the park, playground or school where kids are. Find out where the kids hang out like the pool, the roller rink, the recreation center, or the baseball field.

Making Friends In A New School And Neighborhood

- When you talk to other kids, ask them questions about where they live and what they like to do. What are their favorite sports or their favorite foods? Ask them about school or about their families and pets and hobbies.

- You can ask them to do something with you—go to the park, play catch, go swimming or skate boarding, play a game, jump rope, play some sports, make something, or come over and see your toys.

- If it's okay with your mom and dad, you can invite them to your house to play or eat lunch, or you could visit their houses. You could exchange phone numbers and have them call you or you could call them or send them a note. And later maybe you could have a party and invite some of your classmates, or ask your mom and dad to take you to a movie or to the mall.

- If you try and it doesn't work right away, or if a kid says something mean to you, don't give up and don't get angry or stomp off mad. Try again with someone else. Find other kids who are playing and keep on trying until it works.

- Make yourself easy to like. Relax, be yourself, and act normal. Be open, pleasant, friendly and polite. Be talkative and make yourself visible. Smile, make eye contact, laugh at yourself a little, be witty, and play fair. And most important of all, show kids that you're fun to be with.

Some Tips for Shy Kids

Children who are naturally gregarious or who have been exposed to previous moves or to a variety of social situations often exhibit little reluctance to approach other youngsters or become involved in unfamiliar situations. However most young children, especially those moving for the first time, may display greater hesitation about meeting strangers or interacting with new classmates. Not surprisingly, this is a normal response for kids and for many parents as well. It usually dissipates on its own given a little time.

For children who might be less outgoing and more hesitant to become involved, our "kid experts" offered some additional suggestions to make getting acquainted a little more comfortable. Discussing these tips with your youngsters might help increase their willingness to try other strategies for meeting children and making new friends.

- First of all, try to remember that there is nothing to be afraid of. Loosen up and pretend that you're not shy. It may seem hard to make friends, but it's not.

- Believe in yourself. Just act like you're talking to your mom or dad, or like you did with some of your old friends. It might help you to forget about being shy.

- If you want a friend, you have to show it. Other kids may already have friends or they might be scared, too, so you can't wait for them to make the first move.

- Start out easy, be yourself, and work on being a friend. Pick out some kids who look friendly or a group that you think you might fit in with, and just say "Hi" to them.

- If there are other new kids in your class, sit next to one of them, introduce yourself, smile, act friendly or try to be helpful, or ask them to play at recess. They want to meet people, too.

- Talk to as many kids as you can and try to get to know different kinds of people. Muster your courage, introduce yourself, let people know who you are, and try to find out about them.

- Speak up and talk about yourself in class and on the playground. Try to answer a lot of questions in class or tell

Making Friends In A New School And Neighborhood

good jokes and do something funny in class (but not too funny).

- Do things to make people get interested in you. Be active and fun. Talk about things you like to do or some things you're good at. Teach them a new game or ask them to teach you something.

- Show people that you're interested in them. Join in their sports or games or after school clubs. Try to fit in and behave like them (as long as it's good).

- Ask them to do something with you at school like play a game or work together. Or invite them to your house after school. And if someone asks you to play, do it and don't act shy.

- Most important, be patient and keep trying. If you believe in yourself, other people will like you.

Discussion Tips for Parents

Even though the prospect of making new friends can seem overwhelming to some children, when you talk about it with your youngsters, keep your discussions relatively short, light and fun so that meeting people and making friends becomes an enjoyable opportunity, an adventure rather than the next serious problem to be solved.

You might want to read the suggestions of our "kid experts" with (or to) your children to get their feedback on the ideas they agree with and are willing to try. You can easily use family meeting times, which we discussed in Chapter Four, as a forum for brainstorming ideas on how to meet people and make friends. You might have each child choose one or two listed strategies for meeting others that they feel most comfortable with and are willing to try, and then have them report back on how well they succeeded in their efforts.

Be sure to give them plenty of positive reinforcement for their attempts to meet other children and help them evaluate their "little victories" and the courageous steps they may have taken that week in the getting-acquainted process. Share your own attempts, successes and failures at fitting-in with your youngsters so they can understand that you have experienced feelings and situations similar to theirs.

Finally, if your children are of reading age, you might find it helpful to have them read a children's novel of their choice (see Suggested Fiction for Children, Page 169) describing a fictional youngster's emotions and experiences when faced with the prospect of moving and making friends. You can then use the book and its characters as a basis for discussing your child's feelings.

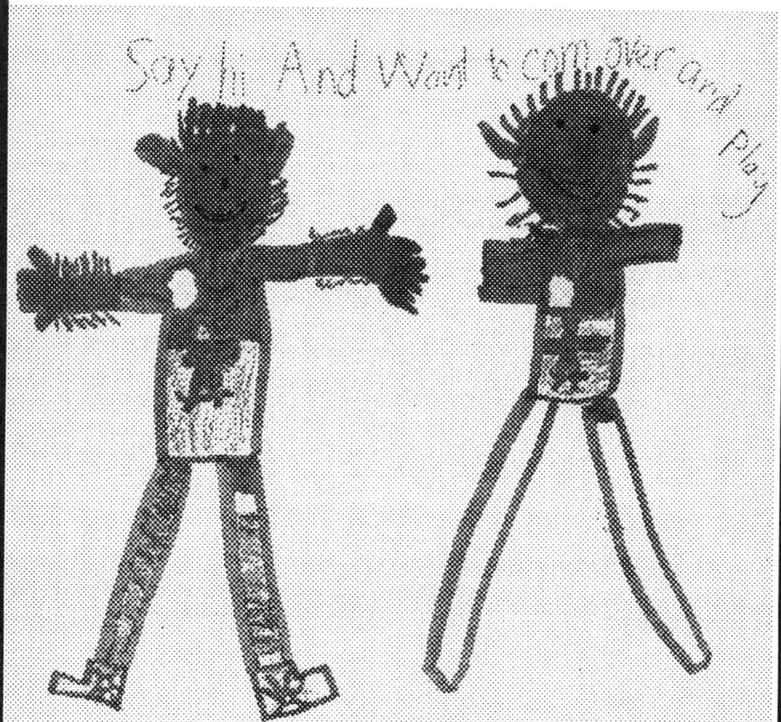
Say hi And Wad to com over and Play

CHAPTER 11

Letters To Roger

When we set out to gather suggestions and practical advice from our "kid experts" for children on the move, we surveyed over 2,500 elementary and middle school youngsters in city schools, suburban schools, rural schools, private schools and even an island school. The kids who responded to our survey shared their ideas with us about moving and making friends on homework assignments, in classroom discussions, creative writing activities, letters, group projects, in drawings, and on tape.

As you can see from the many suggestions presented in Chapters 9 and 12, kids have some very definite thoughts about what works and what doesn't when it comes to being a new kid on the block, exploring unfamiliar territory, and establishing friendships in a new school and neighborhood.

Among the many creative, supportive and caring responses the kids offered were a packet of letters from Ms. Janice Steele's sixth grade students at High Plains Elementary School in Englewood, Colorado. Ms. Steele asked her children to share their ideas on moving and making friends in letters of advice addressed to an imaginary youngster named Roger who had supposedly just moved to their school. The suggestions they offered to Roger were so delightful and potentially helpful to all kids facing similar situations that we wanted you to be able to read and share them with your children for yourselves.

Moving With Children

r,

a common case of "move-itus". Try to talk with
bors or kids living near you. Getting to know one
kid at school will help because he can introduce you to his
friends and so on. Helping people and joining in school activities also works.

Nicholas

* * * * *

Dear Roger,

I can understand how you feel since I have been really shy, too. Instead of thinking that these new people won't be your friends, think about how the other kids would feel if you kept to yourself all the time. Sometimes it may be hard for someone to make friends with you if you never talk to them. Try to be friendly to them. I know it's hard, but try.

Sincerely, Mildred

* * * * *

Dear Roger,

Hi, I'm sorry that you feel this way. I think you should try to be yourself and talk to people. I'm sure that people would love to have you in their group. If those people won't accept you, then try some other kids. I can understand how you feel. But it can't be just them trying, you have to try too.

Sincerely, Fred

* * * * *

Dear Roger,

Since you had friends in your old school, I'm almost positive you can make new friends in this school. It's almost like growing up again. Just try to be yourself and maybe join some clubs. I have a lot of confidence that you can make friends.

Sincerely, John

Letters to Roger

Dear Roger,

I think you need to open up more. Act like you're still in your old school and try to go up and make friends because maybe other kids want to make friends, too.

Yours Truly, Howard

* * * * *

Dear Roger,

I think you should try to sit down with the kids and join in their conversation or just say "Hi." I know you can do it because you've done it before.

Your Friend, Amy

* * * * *

Dear Roger,

If you want to gain friends, here are some things to do:
1. Be kind to everyone.
2. Introduce yourself to people.
3. Enjoy yourself.

Your Friend, Kevin

* * * * *

Dear Roger,

I think even if you only go out there and be friendly and stick out your hand and introduce yourself, you'll have lots of friends.

Truly, Abby

* * * * *

Dear Roger,

Try to be more outgoing and also try to be yourself. Try to act like you did when you were with your old friends. I really had a hard time adjusting to my new neighborhood, but I adjusted just fine. I know you can do it.

Mary

Moving With Children

Dear Roger,

When you see new people, go up to them and just say "Hi" and be real friendly. Don't give up. If it doesn't work, try again and show them that you won't give up trying to be their friend.

Yours Truly, Kerri

* * * * *

Dear Roger,

Don't worry, I'll help you. You should help somebody with their work and maybe if you can, play football and meet them and start talking to them. Go to the next door neighbor and ask him to come to dinner if it's okay with your mom.

Yours Truly, Jeff

* * * * *

Dear Roger,

I think you should be more aggressive. Go up and introduce yourself. Tell them who you are and join clubs and school activities.

Sincerely, Ricky

* * * * *

Dear Roger,

I think you should meet the person next door or across the street with or without your whole family. Walk your dog or ride around the block; and if you see someone, just say "Hi" and introduce yourself.

Caroline

* * * * *

Dear Roger,

There are many things you can do. You can just go with the flow. Do what everyone else is doing. Don't criticize anyone for what they do.

Sincerely, Gina

Dear Roger,

Just try to stay calm and find someone who is nice and considerate and make friends with him. And after a while, you can get to know other people's personalities and then you can make friends with them, too.

Rudy

* * * * *

Dear Roger,

I think you should just talk a lot in class and then you will be noticed.

Sincerely, Takasha

* * * * *

Dear Roger,

Here are some ideas to help you. You could play a lot of sports. You could join activities. Write notes to kids and ask them if they would like to play after school.

Sincerely, Ryan

* * * * *

Dear Roger,

Try to make one very good friend. That friend also has to have friends. After you have made friends with him, you can ask him to show you who his friends are. Meet them and make new friends. To get to know people better; throw a party or a bar-b-que.

Sincerely, Weena

* * * * *

Dear Roger,

I would love to help you in any way possible. If you would like, you can come with me to the movies or to a game when I go. Come over later and I'll introduce you to where my friends and I hang around.

Sincerely, Ryne

Moving With Children

We suggest that you share these letters with your children, either reading to them or having them read some of Roger's mail on their own. Then discuss the suggestions as options for your kids' attempts to become acquainted with people in your new neighborhood.

After reading through the letters together, ask your youngsters what other ideas they might have to help Roger in his getting-acquainted process and which they would be willing to try.

In talking about the recommendations with your kids, make sure to take some time to evaluate and share your own feelings about your new home and neighborhood now that the majority of physical labor of the move is completed.

Ask yourself how many of Roger's tips could benefit you as well as your children. Think about what other advice you might offer to Roger if he were an adult in your position. Finally, be honest with yourself regarding how much of the advice you give your kids you would be willing to follow in order to insure that your move is truly the beginning of a new and enjoyable adventure.

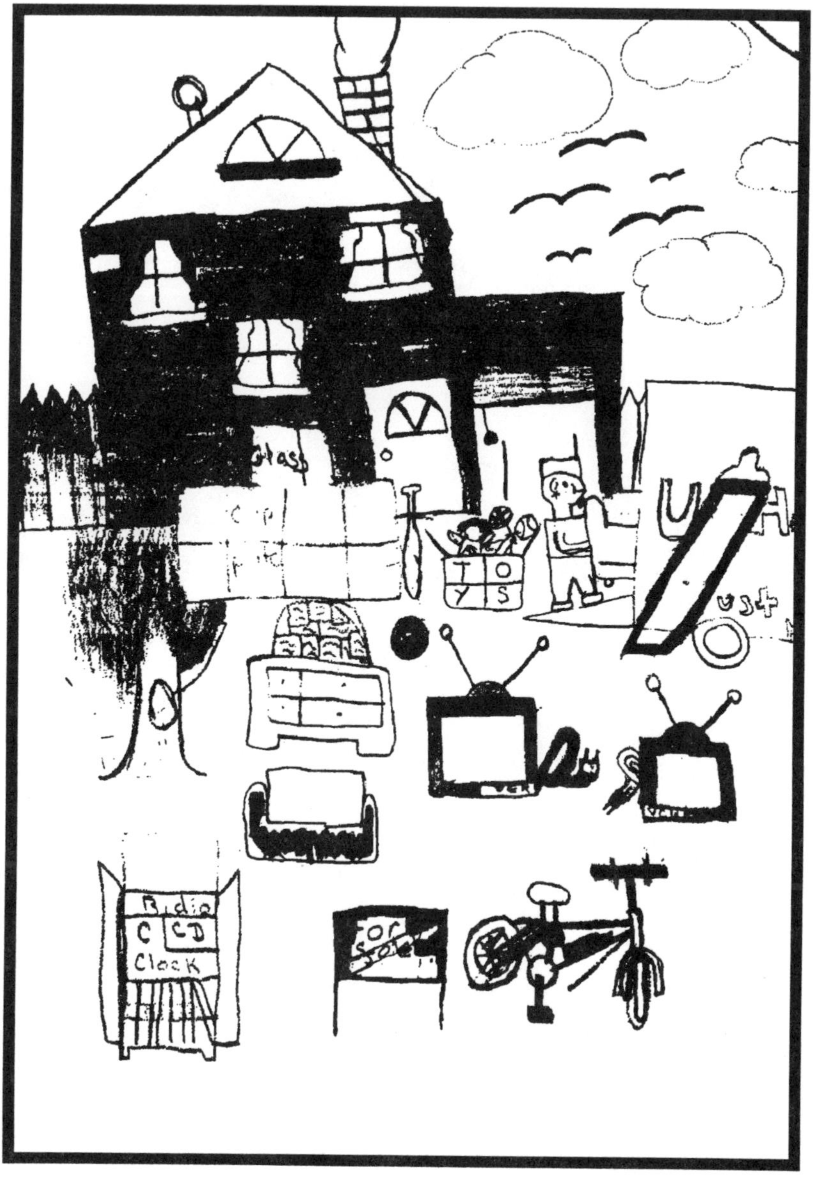
Glass
T O
Y S
C CD
Clock

CHAPTER 12

Some Don'ts About Moving And Making Friends

Perhaps it's only human nature or possibly what we learned as kids by listening to our parents, but it sometimes seems that no matter how positive we try to be when giving advice to our own children, sooner or later we revert to the *don'ts*, that is telling kids what *not* to do as opposed to what we'd like to see them doing. So it isn't the least bit surprising that when our "kid experts" sat down to generate a list of helpful suggestions about making friends for youngsters facing a family move, they eventually slipped in a few *don'ts* of their own. These are the behaviors they felt all kids should avoid when attempting to meet people and establish new friendships.

Unlike most parental admonitions, however, the enjoyable thing about this particular list of kid *don'ts* is that children can in fact produce positive outcomes for themselves by following it. So just as you did with the list of suggestions regarding meeting people and making friends presented in Chapters 10 and 11, take some time to discuss these ideas with your youngsters. To help reassure them that you understand some of the insecurity and awkwardness they may be feeling during this getting-acquainted period, try recalling and sharing with them an example of a humorous "blooper"

...ave made when one of your strategies for making ...iend somehow went awry.

The Don'ts for Kids

According to our "kid experts," here are some definite things children should avoid when setting out to try to meet people and make new friends.

- You *don't* have to do anything special to have a lot of friends, but you have to try at least a little.

- *Don't* worry about being shy. Everyone is shy at first. Try talking. Practice talking to yourself in a mirror or with your family. It's okay to be shy, but if you don't talk to people, you won't have any friends at all.

- *Don't* be too quiet. People won't bite your head off. You can't wait around for kids to approach you. Speak up and *don't* whisper.

- *Don't* be afraid—go out there and introduce yourself to the other kids.

- *Don't* worry if some kids laugh or make fun of you at first because lots of kids tease people they don't know yet.

- *Don't* ignore people. Say nice things to them and *don't* act mean or criticize others.

- *Don't* go on and on about your other school or old friends or how you liked it better before you moved.

- *Don't* try to be something that you're not. Be yourself, and kids will realize that you're a nice person.

- *Don't* act like a hot shot! *Don't* show off or talk about all the stuff you have. *Don't* be a loud mouth. Be cool but not too cool.

Some Don'ts About Moving And Making Friends

- *Don't* act bored. *Don't* play dumb. *Don't* act strange or really silly. *Don't* interrupt. *Don't* be bossy. And *don't* make scenes.

- *Don't* hang around with kids who are troublemakers or bullies.

- Last but not least, *don't* stop—keep talking to kids.

Some Don'ts for Parents

Just as kids learn from adults, parents can probably learn plenty from kids as well. Taking a cue from our "kid experts," we formulated a list of *don'ts* just for parents who are busy working on their own settling-in concerns after the family move. We strongly suggest that you try to avoid all of these *don'ts* (but will certainly understand if you don't) to help make your adjustment to a new home and neighborhood personally enjoyable and rewarding.

- *Don't* get so wrapped up in the details of the move or concerns about your children that you forget to take care of yourself physically or emotionally. Be sure to take some time to relax, to reenergize, and to enjoy yourself.

- *Don't* get so busy with decorating the house, becoming acclimated to a new job, or bogged down with the seemingly endless number of errands to be done that you neglect to give your kids the attention and emotional support they need after the move.

- *Don't* try to accelerate your children's adjustment to or enjoyment of your new surroundings. Give them each the time and space they need to become acquainted and comfortable according to their own personal emotional schedules.

- *Don't* try to resolve all of your kids problems or complaints for them—offer them support, caring and reassurance.

- *Don't* project your fears, concerns or excitement about the move onto your children. Allow them to formulate their own opinions and evaluate their own feelings about your new home and neighborhood.

- *Don't* let your fears and concerns unreasonably limit your children's explorations of unfamiliar territory, new activities or neighborhood companions in which they show an interest. Give them the opportunity to investigate and learn on their own.

- *Don't* pressure your children into situations or activities in which they show no interest or are clearly uncomfortable in the hopes that it will hasten their adjustment.

- *Don't* force your children to maintain cultural habits or fashions from your former home in the new setting unless it seems socially acceptable and appropriate. A sure way to complicate your child's adjustment process, for example, is to insist that he wear his Cleveland Browns tee-shirt into a Denver classroom just because you are a loyal fan.

- *Don't* force children to "make a choice" between the old and the new by constantly comparing your new home and community with the one you've just left.

- *Don't* burden your youngsters' attempts at adjustment to new surroundings with memories of the past by constantly reminiscing about or "missing" old friends and neighbors. Allow yourself to say goodbye so that you can really begin your new adventure.

Some Don'ts About Moving And Making Friends

- *Don't* create greater anxiety or concern for your children by suggesting worries about the new neighborhood or school they may not have as yet considered.

- *Don't* feel as if you must always have the right advice or perfect solutions for all getting-acquainted dilemmas— offer your children the freedom to test their adjustment strategies and to fail on their own.

- *Don't* get overly involved in all of your children's new activities.

- *Don't fool yourself into believing that the success of your move depends on your children's immediate adjustment and happiness. It will come in time at its own pace.*

Moving With Children

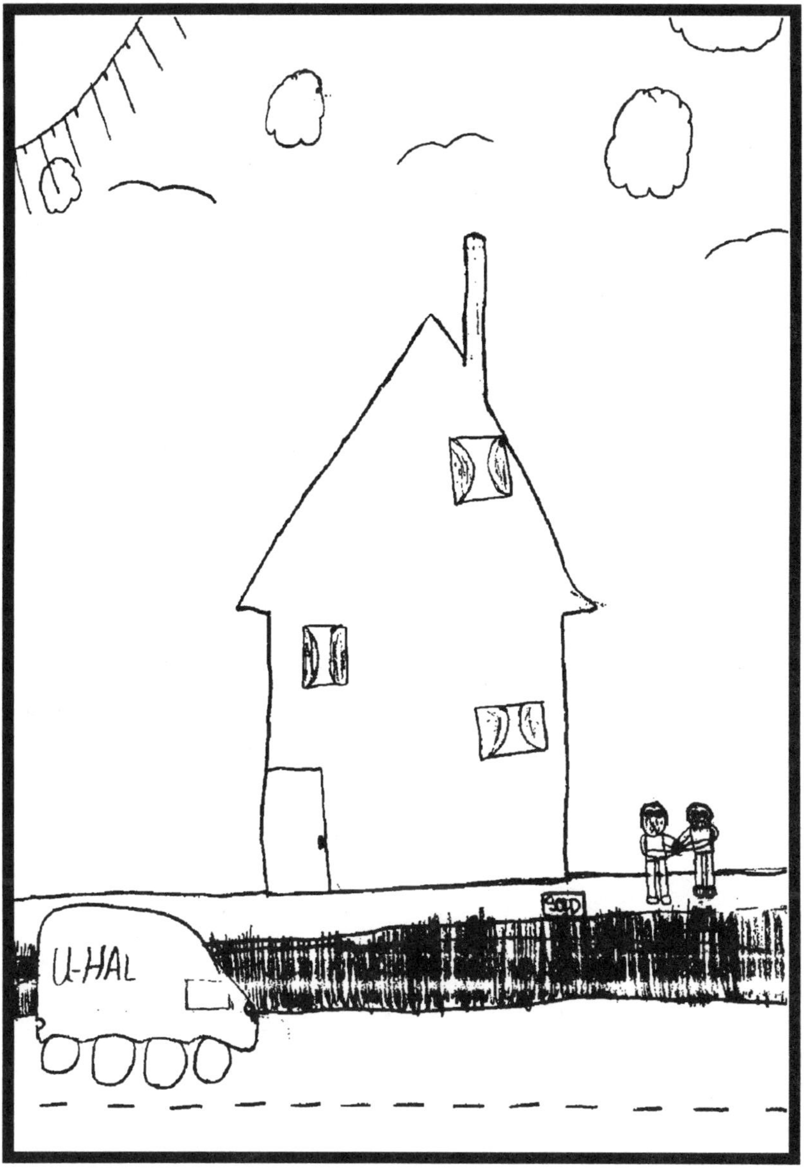
U-HAL
SOLD

CHAPTER 13

What Kids Want From Parents

So far, we have presented our advice for parents about helping kids enjoy the family's moving adventure. We've shared suggestions for kids from kids about exploring a new neighborhood and making friends, presented ideas for parents on reducing stress and taking care of themselves during the arduous process of a family move, and given tips for dealing with the family's feelings about relocating. Now we would like to tell you what kids say they would like from adults after a move.

As part of the moving survey, we asked our "kid experts" the question, "If you moved to a new school or a new neighborhood, what do you think your parents or your teachers could do to help you meet new people and make friends?" In their responses, the kids offered a diversity of opinions as well as some worthwhile advice.

A small number of somewhat independent-minded children strongly expressed the belief that the process of meeting people and making new friends is strictly "kid business" meant to be handled by children without adult involvement. One youngster, Kenny, a fourth grader, proclaimed, "If I moved to a new school, I would want my parents to let things happen by themselves because sometimes that's the best thing to do." A third grader named Jake seconded that opinion with the comment, "I wouldn't really need help. I would like to make friends on my own."

Naturally if your child exhibits such an independent attitude and handles unfamiliar situations well on her or his own, you can best reinforce your youngster's self-reliance by providing encouragement and support in more indirect and less active ways, such as simply being available and willing to talk or giving suggestions when your child seeks you out for assistance.

It is important, however, to stay alert for the various behavioral and verbal signals of distress: dissatisfaction or anger with the neighborhood or school, new and illogical fears, sadness, negativism, sleeplessness, nightmares, a reluctance to be away from home or family, a significant drop in school performance or a loss of interest in previously enjoyed activities, which might indicate that a youngster is having difficulty becoming comfortable with her or his new surroundings after a move. Should these signs begin to appear, you can then step in to offer your child more active guidance and support in the adjustment process.

A second group of children indicated that parental help would be most welcomed in the form of emotional and verbal support and encouragement. The kids stated that parents could help simply by asking questions, discussing feelings, and making suggestions. They also felt that parents could encourage them to meet new friends and try new activities by giving them the permission and freedom to explore their new surroundings. John, a sixth-grader, summed up the sentiments of many children by saying, "I'd want my mom to understand how I feel about moving and losing my old friends. And I'd just want her to talk to me about it and sort of comfort me.

In reality all children faced with a new or stressful situation like a family move need and want this form of parental support but are sometimes reluctant or unsure about asking for it. By answering questions, discussing and sharing feelings, and offering reassurance, you'll find all family members better able to deal with the settling-in process in a more comfortable and less stressful manner.

What Kids Want From Parents

The third and largest group of children we surveyed welcomed even greater and more active parental involvement during the settling-in and getting-acquainted stage of the move. In response to the question of what they would like from parents, the kids offered the following suggestions they thought would be helpful for them:

- Parents could help by meeting the neighbors, finding out if they had kids my age, then taking me to meet them.

- My parents and I could go for walks in the neighborhood and introduce ourselves to any kids around.

- Parents could take us to different places where the kids and other families hang out to see if there are any kids we might like.

- Mom or dad could walk me to school for the first few days so I got to know the way, and they could help me talk to the other kids.

- My folks could invite other people with kids over so that I could spend time with them to get a feel for what they are like while the adults are talking.

- Parents could help me join a club at school or get me involved in a sports team or some other activity where I could meet kids my age.

- They could let me invite other kids over to play, for a snack, a lunch or a picnic or maybe take us all to the movies.

- Parents could invite all the neighbors over for a cookout or a pot luck with their kids. Or they could let me have a party for all the kids before school starts.

If your child does appear to be experiencing difficulty taking the initiative or seems to be having little success in meeting other neighborhood or school children, keep in mind that your task is not to go out and make friends for your youngster, but to help create an atmosphere that will encourage your child to establish new friendships.

Try discussing the ideas presented by our "kid experts" as possible starting points for meeting the neighbor kids. Offer them as suggestions and follow up on those that seem agreeable and comfortable to your child. Don't push a specific idea or activity that appeals to you, however, if your child is not comfortable with it.

Remember that this list represents only a small sampling of ideas and is meant to stimulate your family's brainstorming powers to create your own imaginative plan for getting acquainted with your neighbors and making new friends.

Some Other Things Parents Can Do for Kids

In looking at the kids' list of ideas regarding how parents can help during the settling-in stage of the move, it is obvious that most children perceive a parent's assistance as falling into the category of exploring the neighborhood and helping a child figure out where other kids congregate. From a more adult point of view, however, there are some other practical steps a parent can take to help ease a child through the settling-in process.

If your child has any special educational or medical needs, such as a learning or physical disability, begin checking out resources (see Resource Organizations for Families, Page 174) long before your move so that neither of you will have to experience a disruption in meeting those needs after the move.

If your child has exceptional skills or talents or a unique interest, investigate local groups and organizations which offer appropriate activities or lessons.

Keep in mind that preschool youngsters have little opportunity and don't possess the social skills to meet and develop friendships with neighborhood children on their own, so you may have to be more involved to the extent of spending regular times at the playground or inviting neighbor children over until your child feels comfortable and familiar enough to seek out other youngsters.

You may also find that a nursery or day care center offers your preschool youngster greater opportunities than an individual babysitter for prolonged interactions with other children in your area. Day care arrangements can also lead to friendships both for you and your child.

If your child is of school age, arrange for an orientation tour of the elementary or middle school. Meet your child's teachers and acquaint them with any special educational needs, strengths or interests that your child might possess.

Some schools provide "welcome" groups and special activities to introduce new students to their classes. If your child's school offers such a program, help your youngster compile information and photographs about him or herself, your family, and your previous home to share with classmates.

If your youngster seems to be having an exceptionally difficult time getting acquainted and meeting friends, ask for assistance from the elementary or middle school counselors, who frequently help new students through the initial stages of the adjustment process.

Finally, keep in mind that turn about is fair play. If youngsters feel they can request that you accompany them on their initial explorations of the neighborhood or take them to the park so they can meet other children, it only seems fair that you can take kids to the recreation center or the ice cream shop in the hopes of meeting other adults on the block. As a matter of fact, it not only seems fair but could be fun for all of you.

In closing this chapter, we wish to reiterate that a successful family move is a matter of teamwork between parents and children. Your children will look to you for assistance and support, but they may not always ask for it directly and at times will want to handle things on their own. But they will also watch to see how you go about the settling-in process and follow your lead. Your task is to lay the foundation for a successful move.

EMMAUS PUBLIC LIBRARY
11 E. MAIN STREET
EMMAUS, PA 18049

CHAPTER 14

Going To A New School

Without a doubt, one of the most important and, at times, most stressful adjustments children face when a family moves is becoming comfortable in a new school. Youngsters worry about finding their way around, meeting new classmates, adjusting to a new teacher, understanding school rules, and being able to handle academic expectations.

Research findings from Denver's Piton Foundation (10) indicate that changing schools can play a significant role in a youngster's academic success. Their statistics demonstrate that children who attend a single elementary, middle and high school tend to score better on standardized achievement tests and exhibit a significantly higher graduation rate than those who who change schools even once during their basic educational years.

Our own first-hand experiences as members of a school mental health team also demonstrate that schools differ tremendously in the amount of energy and effort they devote to helping new students become integrated into the school community. Some schools with highly transient student populations are often more familiar with the difficulties that confront children who experience school changes and offer orientation activities designed to acquaint students with their new surroundings. In contrast, schools in well established communities that undergo far fewer student transfers often pay less attention to the needs of new students.

Even individual classroom teachers within the same building can exhibit vastly different approaches to the introduction of new students into their classes. Some teachers regularly employ specially designed games, activities and introduction strategies to help children get to know their new classmates. Others require students to take more personal initiative and responsibility for their own getting-acquainted process. Naturally the amount of attention a new student receives from any given teacher can be influenced by the time of the school year that the child enters the classroom, the school activities occurring at the time a child transfers, or simply the teacher's awareness of a new student's needs.

The first important step toward integrating your child in a new school is to visit the school together to meet the principal and teachers and to tour the building. The points of greatest interest and concern for most children are the location of:

- the bus stops,
- the doors they should use to enter the building,
- their classrooms,
- the storage areas for coats and lunches,
- the bathrooms,
- the cafeteria, gym and media center or library,
- the principal's office,
- the playground areas their class uses.

Depending on your child's age, it would also be wise to plan on walking along to school or to the bus stop for at least the first week to help your youngster become accustomed to the routine.

In talking with teachers and children about the Moving Survey, we discovered that teachers could encourage greater sensitivity among students to the needs of new classmates simply by discussing the five survey questions in their classrooms. One specific suggestion you can make to your child's

Going To A New School

teachers is that these or similar questions be addressed in some form of classroom discussion or activity.

In addition to that however, our "kid experts" indicated that teachers might also want to try some of the following strategies for helping kids become comfortable in a new classroom:

- Teachers should always tell you what the school rules are. They should show you where to find things like the library and the bathroom, and they should tell you early when your first test will be.

- Teachers could get one of your new classmates to sit and talk with you and show you around and tell you about some of the things that go on in class. Or the teacher could pair you up with a buddy or with a different kid each day until you know your way around.

- Teachers could introduce you to the class and ask kids to include you in games at recess or eat lunch with you.

- The teacher could let you go up in front of the room so that you could tell the kids about yourself, and the other kids could ask you questions or tell you something about themselves.

- Teachers could help by letting you talk to people in class so you can get a feel for what they are like or introduce you to the kids you might have something in common with.

- Or they could have you do some fun activities to get to know the other kids, like wear name tags or maybe have a class party; or maybe the teacher could move you around the room so you get a chance to sit by everybody and get to know them.

Some Tips for Teachers

Some of the teachers who responded to our Moving Survey also included the following strategies they have found effective in helping new students become comfortable in their classrooms. You might share this list of ideas with your child's teacher as well.

- Before a new student arrives in class, conduct a classroom discussion announcing that a new student will be coming and talk about things that children can do to make her or him feel welcome.

- Help children feel expected and welcome by having their desks, name tags, workbooks and materials ready for them when they arrive.

- Supply new parents with brief list of classroom rules and procedures along with a class list of students' names, addresses and phone numbers with information about which parents are involved in various school-related activities.

- Appoint a student welcoming committee or a series of classroom buddies who could familiarize the new child with the school and the rules, procedures, and expectations of the classroom.

- Briefly touch base with the new student each morning and afternoon to answer questions, offer reassurance and check to see how she or he is coming along in the settling-in process.

- When possible, utilize team projects or assignments so the child can work with a small group of students until she or he is more familiar with classroom procedures.

When teachers incorporate ideas such as these, a child's apprehension about entering a new school will dissipate quickly as they begin to perceive themselves as integral

Going To A New School

members of the classroom. These techniques can lessen a parent's fears about a new school, and they will reinforce the idea that children, parents and teachers are all working together to insure a child's success in a new school.

Moving With Children

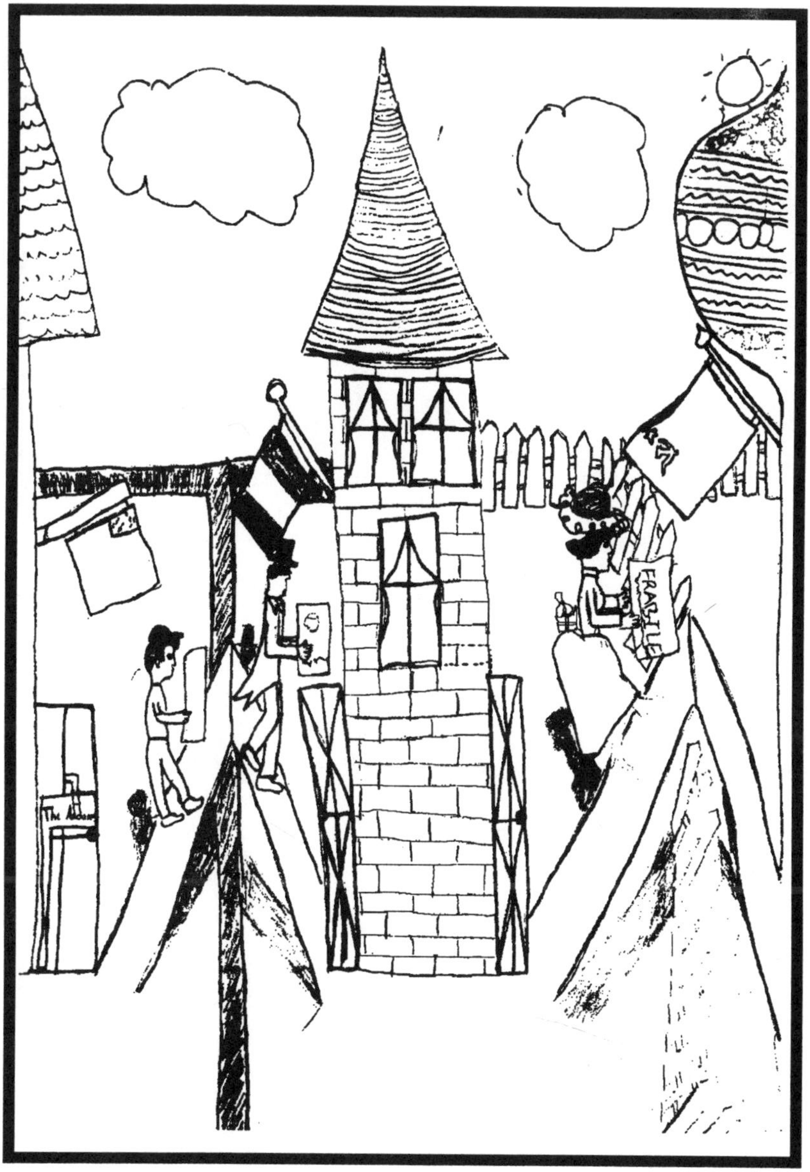

CHAPTER 15

The Million-mile Move: Moving To A Foreign Country

Moving to a new home should always be an adventure, but relocating to a new country may be the most exciting and stressful undertaking a family will ever share. Though the standard home atlas defines the circumference of the earth as just under 25,000 miles, any move outside a youngster's familiar boundaries can seem almost that far. It shouldn't be surprising then that a move to a foreign country may feel like a million miles or more.

Whether your family moves for business, religious, military, educational, social or philosophical reasons and unless your destination is one of a handful of major cities worldwide, the announcement of your move to a foreign country is bound to be greeted by the question, "Where's that?" Your kids won't be the only ones asking the question either. You can expect it from friends, relatives, co-workers, neighbors, casual acquaintances and, perhaps most troublesome of all, a little voice in the back of your own head that repeatedly asks, "Now where is it we're moving to?"

A move to a foreign country is one of the more stressful times in a family's life according to Dr. Ruth A. Bleuzé, Director of Training at Moran, Stahl and Boyer, a Boulder-based firm specializing in counseling families who are relocating overseas for business purposes. She says that a foreign move is a "quantum leap" compared to any domestic relocation, and its success depends on the cohesiveness of the family members and how well they know how to communicate with and rely on each other for support.

If your family is considering a move to a foreign port of call, keep in mind that all of the practical, social and emotional issues we have discussed become magnified in a cross cultural move, and a myriad of new concerns appears as well. The preparation stage prior for a foreign move presents an unlimited supply of unknowns for the entire family with an infinite array of details to be handled, problems to be solved, anxieties to be allayed, and questions to be answered of which "Where's that?" is only the first.

In cross cultural moves, families must learn to understand, if not speak, the basic phrases of a foreign language or at least the regional slang and common idioms of other English-speaking countries. They must become familiar with local customs, taboos and dress. They must learn to eat unusual foods and trade in foreign currency, adjust to different school systems and acclimate to vastly different weather and geographic conditions.

For example Americans who relocate to Iceland must learn to make change in *kronur* and grow accustomed to long periods of darkness during the winter and almost endless daylight in the summer. They become wary of "black ice" on the roads, high wind warnings that require children under fifty pounds to be picked up from school by their parents, and they learn to savor hot dogs made from lamb.

Moving to Bermuda means adjusting to driving on the left side of the road and having national law dictate the maximum size of the car you drive. It also means dressing your children in standardized school uniforms and learning to deal with high humidity, frequent rains, giant cockroaches, occasional hurricane warnings, coral scrapes and jellyfish stings.

The Million-mile Move:
Moving To A Foreign Country

Many of your children's questions about the family's destination will reflect your own concerns about this strange new place where you have chosen to live. They may range from the practical, "Do they play baseball there?" "Will there be peanut butter and pizza?" and "Do they have television?" to the more worrisome, "Will we still be Americans?" "Can we ever come back home?" and "What will we do if there's a war?" Regardless of how insignificant some of the questions might sound, they all represent concerns that each family member may need reassurance about.

In Chapter 1 we stated that effective planning and preparation, cooperation and working together, sharing feelings and concerns, and giving each other assurance, comfort and support are vital ingredients in making your move a positive experience for the entire family. Nowhere is that more true than in a move to a foreign country, says Dr. Bleuzé, whose training programs focus on strengthening family communication, problem-solving and support skills.

Though most foreign relocations centered around educational and business pursuits or religious or military service transfers include some form of orientation to the host country, working together as a family team throughout the move is a required passport for your family's successful sojourn in a foreign land.

A basic tenet of the Moran, Stahl and Boyer training program is "work together and get as much information as you can." Assuming that no one in your family is an "expert" on the country you are moving to, a simple way to begin your family's cross cultural orientation program is to pretend that you are all tourists with absolutely no idea of what lies ahead. This means treating all questions about your destination as something everyone in the family should know.

Utilize a portion of your Message Moving Board (Chapter 4) to list any questions that come to mind and discuss them as a group during your family meeting time. This simple strategy can accomplish several important objectives. First, it reinforces the idea of family teamwork and support. Second, it helps remove doubts, calm fears and share helpful information; and perhaps most important, it can stimulate questions regarding what else you all need to discover about your new destination.

A simplified adaptation of the ancient adage that the longest journey begins with a single step may be that a move halfway around the world begins with a trip to your local library or bookstore. There you can obtain a variety of information dealing with the history, geography, social and political climate of your new country, not to mention travel guides, maps and globes, foreign language books, magazines, newspapers, tapes and ethnic cookbooks.

A world map or globe along with a detailed map of your new country can provide your destination with a real sense of place in relation to your present home as well as other geographic areas your family may have visited. Referring to the maps as you continue to gather information and answer questions also instills a greater sense of predictability and control about the move that can help ease feelings of anxiety and uncertainty.

Speak with as many people as you can who may have visited or lived in your destination country. If your move is the result of a business, religious service or military transfer, talk to colleagues who may have preceded you in similar assignments. Contact the travel editor of your local newspaper or a librarian at the nearest library for articles and books regarding your destination. Instructors in the history and foreign-language departments of your community high school or local college can also be excellent resources. Some larger communities have social organizations for various ethnic groups, and many states maintain honorary consuls to countries around the world who would be delighted with your interest in the countries they represent.

Tourist travel guides are tremendously helpful tools for becoming acquainted with a new country. Because they are

The Million-mile Move:
Moving To A Foreign Country

written for readers who may not have a great deal of time to do research on their destinations, they present a great deal of useful information in a concise manner. Most travel guides offer a summary of a country's history, an overview of its present social/political situation, rules and regulations for foreign visitors, local laws, currency exchange, travel, public transportation, health and weather information, points of interest, places to eat and shop and local maps. The best guides will also pique your interest by offering descriptions of the people and customs as well as handy tips to help you deal with immediate needs and potentially embarrassing situations.

During a teaching assignment in Keflavik, Iceland one of the authors was forever grateful for his well-worn copy of *Iceland in a Nutshell* (11). Besides providing the necessary travel information and a comforting list of the various labels one might expect on restroom doors, this pocket companion offered the following gems: Icelanders enjoy public debate and often argue loudly in restaurants and on street corners simply because they enjoy the interaction. They, like many Europeans, never stand in line so do not be surprised if you are shouldered aside by children or senior citizens while waiting for buses or entering buildings. And if you look away even for a second, servers in restaurants will whisk away your delicious Icelandic bread regardless of how much of it remains on your plate before a meal.

Visit your local video rental store for foreign-language movies with subtitles or travel tapes. Check with the museum of natural history or a local travel group to see if they offer films or slide presentations on your host country. Investigate the many informational and foreign-language cable television channels, some of which offer cartoons and children's programming in foreign languages. Finally, don't overlook popular movies that may have been filmed in foreign locations.

Be creative with your family in using the time before your move to practice, practice, practice. Practice the language, practice with the currency, and practice with the food.

Most bookstores and libraries offer foreign-language audiotapes for both children and adults, and some also stock foreign-language versions of familiar children's books such as *Dr. Seuss, The Berenstain Bears* and *Sesame Street* to provide an enjoyable introduction to a different language for youngsters. The same is true for various popular magazines and even comic books. Foreign-language music and song tapes can also be obtained at most record stores.

Some specialty stores carry wrist watches with numbers spelled out in foreign languages as well as foreign-language placemats and tee-shirts imprinted with everyday greetings and useful expressions with the correct pronunciations spelled out in English below each phrase. For a combination of learning and family fun, French, British, German and Russian-language versions of *Monopoly* are also available.

Many large banks, major airports and coin shops offer a cash exchange service where you can purchase foreign currency. Obtain a variety of small bills and change to provide your family practice in handling foreign money or give the kids their allowances in foreign currency so they can become familiar with exchange rates by trading it in for American dollars and cents before they spend it on their favorite purchases.

If there are any ethnic restaurants in your area, plan a few family dinners during which you can sample the various tastes you will be experiencing in your new home. If there are none available, get an ethnic cookbook from your bookstore or library, prepare some foreign foods and pretend that your meal is being served in a local restaurant in a foreign country where you have to practice speaking the language and paying for your meal in foreign currency.

These strategies won't guarantee you a completely worry-free arrival at a foreign destination but they will help all of

The Million-mile Move:
Moving To A Foreign Country

you become more familiar with some of the situations you may encounter along the way. With this familiarity also comes a greater sense of predictability and control that can only help ease some of the anxieties you will all experience as you set out on your journey to a foreign country.

Packing prior to your departure for a new country presents a unique combination of practical and emotional hurdles for families that require special attention from parents. To some extent immigration laws in most countries limit the amount and nature of personal possessions that can be brought into a country. They may also severely restrict or completely ban the importation of animals. The mere logistics and costs of foreign relocation also govern how much families can take with them, so many prized possessions, including pets, which could easily be packed and moved during a domestic relocation may get left behind.

For most families this means parting, either temporarily or forever, with many familiar artifacts taken for granted as a part of everyday life—furniture, automobiles, power tools and cookware as well as more personal and emotionally cherished items such as your cookbook collection, the 400 murder mysteries you plan to reread or that new set of cross country skis you were learning to use. For kids it might mean leaving behind a favorite bunkbed, a treasured rock collection, a beat-up mountain bike, or the family dog. Even if you can move some of them with you, another simple truth about foreign relocations is that most of these prized possessions will arrive at your destination many months after you do.

Whether the separation from these implements of daily living is permanent or only temporary, it produces a sense of loss for you and your children that is important to recognize and talk about. It is not only a loss of possessions that contribute to your comfort and enjoyment of everyday life but a partial loss of personal identity which you will experience much more intensely during a foreign move than a domestic one where we can carry the majority of our belongings and our identities with us.

Because of this sense of loss, parents will need to be more involved in helping children make decisions about what can be taken and what must be left behind. Talking about your destination country and what may or may not be available, necessary or appropriate there long before you begin packing can make some decisions easier for children. Be creative about dealing with the possessions you decide to leave behind. Talk to your kids about making a donation of furniture, clothing, toys and recreational equipment to a local nursery, day care or treatment center or shelter for the homeless. The pain of leaving cherished possessions behind may be partially replaced by the pride of having helped others in need.

Look at different options for housing those items your child wishes to keep for the future but that cannot be taken along. Ask relatives or close friends if they would act as guardians for your child's possessions so she or he will feel they are in safe hands. You might also gather a number of the smaller items—books, small toys, stuffed animals, collections, games—and arrange to have a relative or friend send one to your child as a surprise for special occasions such as birthdays or holidays. You might try this for yourself as well. Imagine your delight if you were to open a package from home to discover a favorite book, a small piece of jewelry or a collection of photographs you had decided to leave behind.

Help your child choose one familiar object to represent a special piece of "home" to carry with you as you travel to your new destination. This tangible symbol of "home" can help reduce the sense of loss children experience by offering a bit of security and comfort, and it can act as an emotional bridge between your old and your new homes.

Finally and perhaps most difficult, foreign moves most often mean that pets must be left behind. The emotional attachment some families have for their pets can result in intense feelings of loss for the entire family not unlike those accompanying the death of a loved one. In such situations parents must make extra efforts to recognize and help children understand, deal with and accept their feelings of loss and grief about the necessity to give up a pet because of the move. Because of the emotional significance of such a loss, we invite you to review once again the discussion of leaving pets behind in the section on *Special Goodbyes for Special Moves* in Chapter 6.

Getting There is Part of the Job

In any move the actual amount of time spent traveling from one place to the next is a relatively small portion of the overall moving process. Most of us have experienced at least one local move in which we've finished loading the moving van, jumped into our cars, arrived at new houses and started unpacking all in less than hour. During a foreign relocation however, traveling long distances with your family to a far-off destination can become an arduous ordeal that requires a hefty supply of parental understanding, patience and imagination. It is also a good time to remind yourself that the more comfortable and in-control you can remain, the more successful the trip will be for all of you.

Even if your children have been blessed with the uncanny ability to sleep anywhere and under almost any conditions, the odds are that you haven't. Make sure that you are all relaxed and well rested before beginning your journey. If necessary, spend a night with friends or in a quiet hotel so that you can get a good night's sleep before your first day of travel. Take time to go over whatever clothing, toiletries and miscellaneous supplies you will be carrying with you—at least enough to last each of you two days in case of misplaced luggage. Spend some quiet time together talking about your feelings and hopes for what lies ahead. Your adventure has begun.

On your day of departure plan ahead to enjoy a good meal and an easy trip to the airport with plenty of time to get the luggage checked, purchase a last few odds-and-ends at the gift shop and find your gate. The last things you need before setting off are a hurried meal, traffic jams, and frustrated scurrying as you try to find your way around the airport with the kids in tow. Once you've accomplished all that, however, you might as well sit back and begin practicing your patience since the passwords for much international travel seem to be *wait* and *delay*.

In addition to the physical rigors of long-distance travel, you can expect to encounter inevitable delays and a change in the pace at which you and your family may be accustomed to doing things. International travel offers numerous factors that may slow your progress—unfamiliar airport procedures, foreign languages both in spoken and printed form, crowds of travelers from different countries, customs checks and security precautions. To weary travelers these may not only seem unreasonable but usually raise everyone's stress levels. Try to take these experiences in stride and use them as opportunities to observe and learn so that as you become more familiar with them, you will also feel more comfortable and confident in your ability to deal with whatever may lie ahead.

Adjusting to a New Culture

Once you arrive at your overseas destination, a whole new array of surprises awaits. According to the Moran, Stahl and Boyer overseas relocation training guide (12), all families moving to a foreign destination eventually experience some form of culture shock as a result of a slow build-up of stress caused by having to deal with unfamiliar situations on a daily basis. Simple tasks that you take for granted at home—grocery shopping, making phone calls, greeting people on the street or going out to dinner—may suddenly seem difficult and at times overwhelming simply because they are done so differently or perhaps not at all in your host country.

Culture shock is not a problem that one develops and recovers from nor does it appear suddenly as the result of a single event. It is a slow build-up of stresses caused by an accumulation of different incidents, some major and others rela-

The Million-mile Move: Moving To A Foreign Country

tively minor, that seem to grind away at expectation and comfort levels without your awareness. One way to relieve some of the stress on yourself and your family is simply to recognize that feeling anxious, although unwelcome, is a normal experience for anyone adjusting to life in a foreign culture.

What we call culture shock can also be viewed as a cycle of readjustment with four fairly predictable phases.

Phase 1: This initial phase of a foreign relocation is one filled with excitement and an enthusiastic spirit of adventure in which you are likely to act much like a tourist, taking lots of photographs and enjoying all the new and different things you encounter.

Phase 2: During the second phase of your readjustment, which can last for several months, elements of the foreign culture which you initially found enchanting become bothersome and can produce irritation, impatience, frustration, anger and depression. The intensity of these feelings may cause family bickering, interfere with work performance or school adjustment, or generate withdrawn, obsessive or overtly hostile behaviors toward your host country.

Phase 3: Families who remain in a foreign country, despite the trials and tribulations of Phase 2, eventually learn to change and adapt to local customs and behaviors. Their feelings of isolation diminish; they feel more comfortable, regain their self-confidence and begin looking toward the future.

Phase 4: In this final phase of the cycle of readjustment you and your family will eventually begin to feel at home and come to enjoy and appreciate your host country and its culture.

Culture shock, especially Phase 2, can be a difficult process for families to deal with, but knowing in advance the pattern of phases you are likely to experience and facing them as a family team can help you deal with them more effectively as they arise.

According to Dr. Bleuzé the most important focus of the Moran, Stahl and Boyer overseas training program is helping families realize that they will experience periods of stress during which they will be one another's sole support system. She and her staff work to strengthen the positive ways in which families can help each other through the stressful times of foreign relocation so they can fully enjoy their experiences in a foreign culture.

Among the many family strategies included in the training program are:

- setting goals and making agreements about discussing and dealing with stress issues once families reach their destination

- creating times for structured family activities and rituals to strengthen togetherness and teamwork

- structuring ways of keeping in touch with friends, relatives and other support persons back home

- working together on a family journal, travel guide or adventure album that includes lists of things they've learned, people they've met, places they've visited, foods they've tried, friends they've made, "little victories" and "tiny failures", and the problems they've confronted and solved together along the way

Any move can be difficult for a family, and the emotional labor involved in an overseas family relocation can sometimes seem overwhelming. Adjusting to life in another country can be extremely stressful and at times even frightening. With adequate preparation, support, communication and teamwork however, a "million-mile move" can bring families closer together, help them mature, expand their horizons and enrich their lives by providing one of the most exciting and rewarding experiences a family can share.

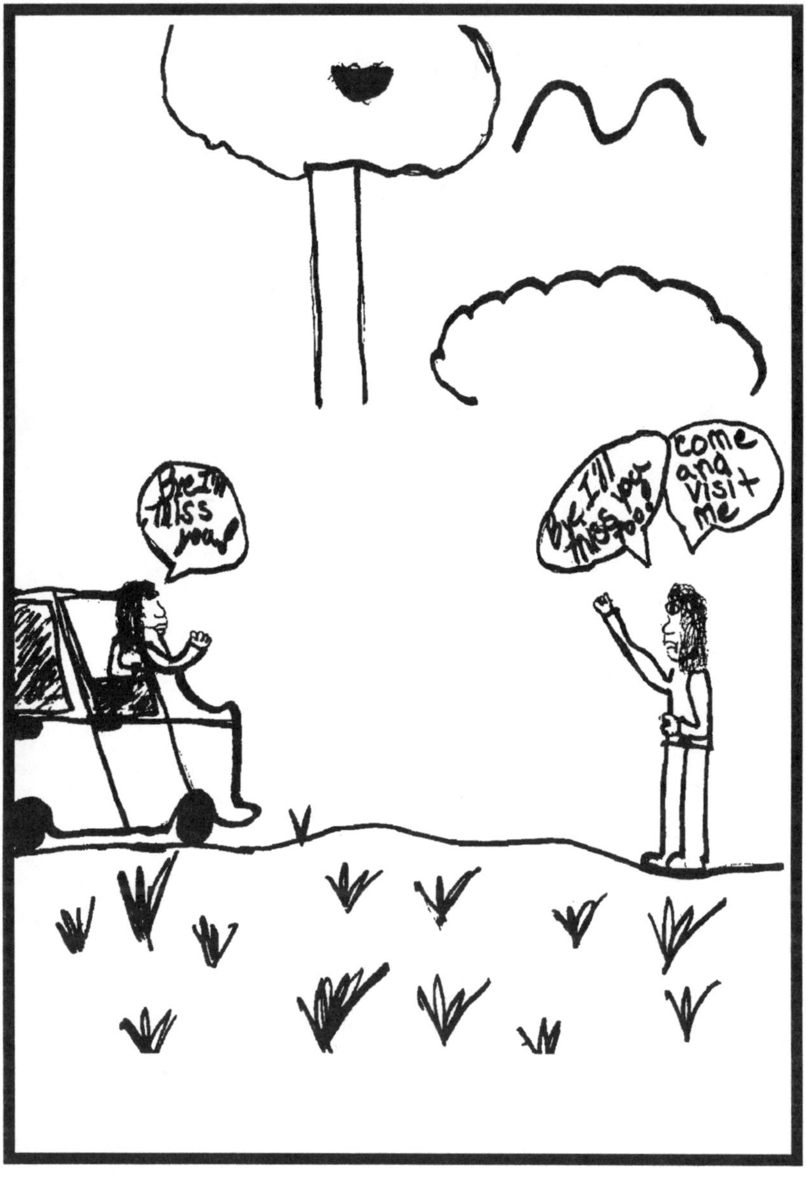
Bye I'll miss you!
Bye I'll miss you too!
come and visit me

CHAPTER 16

Some Final Thoughts About Moving

Estimates vary on the average length of time it might take for a family to settle in completely following a move, with typical projections falling anywhere between six months to a year-and-half for the average family. In looking at your own moving experience, it is important to remember that feelings of loss, disorientation, fear, stress, anger, doubt and uncertainty are all natural for anyone faced with the enormity of life change that a move presents. Simply being in new surroundings without easy access to familiar faces can produce doubts about a person's self-worth and sense of identity, and it is best to realize that it may take some time before a salesperson calls you by name, a waitress accepts your check without requesting identification, or a local community group recognizes your many organizational or artistic abilities.

Being aware of these feelings in yourself can only help in recognizing and dealing with those of your children. Their feelings will parallel and, in some cases, be expressed more openly than yours, but this, too, is natural for children. Straight A students may feel "dumb" and out of place in a new school, an all-star shortstop will worry about being able to make the team or resent sitting on the bench with unfamiliar teammates, and a usually gregarious youngster may experience anxiety at the thought of meeting neighbor children for the first time.

A great majority of these scary feelings, both yours and your children's, will dissipate naturally over time as you find your way around and take the opportunities to exhibit your unique talents and skills. Operating as a family team is one of the most effective ways to speed up the adjustment process and reduce the amount of emotional disruption a move might cause.

In some situations where time alone doesn't seem to alleviate the difficulties caused by a move, we encourage you to consider the multitude of potential resources available to parents and families that might be of help to you during the settling-in period. Ask your realtor, sometimes a family's first contact with a new neighborhood or community, for information about social, religious, educational, cultural, and professional activities in your area. Obtain information, usually at no cost, from your moving company, the chamber of commerce, newcomers' services, co-workers and employers, the local church of your affiliation, your children's school, and local or national service organizations that might help your family feel more comfortable and adjust more quickly to your new home.

Although most children and families will never require professional help in dealing with their feelings about moving, there are cases in which a child's unhappiness or fears about a move may become more disruptive or persist for a period longer than a parent might consider reasonable. A child's sense of grief and loss over the move may trigger unresolved feelings from an earlier loss, feelings that a parent feels unequipped to handle. In such instances the child may need professional counseling.

For parents in search of such help, the first step is to ask your child's teacher for information during the adjustment process. Today most public schools have available school psychologists, social workers or counselors, many of whom often deal with "newcomer" situations.

Some Final Thoughts About Moving

Should parents prefer the services of a mental health professional outside the school system, a school psychologist, social worker, nurse or counselor can usually refer them to professionals in the immediate area. Parents can also receive help through a local mental health or medical center or by contacting the community psychological or social work organization for names of licensed professionals in the community. In most cases such professional intervention should yield positive results for families in a fairly short period of time.

Don't be too surprised if there are times following the move when everyone in the family seems happy and excited about your new home *except* you. In relocating your family you have taken on a big responsibility, and it is not uncommon for the person in charge to feel an emotional let-down after completing a major project. Experiencing "the blues," a feeling of emptiness or loss, or even a short period of depression is a natural response to a move once the kids are back in school and everyone gets into a familiar routine. Taking action is the best solution for beating "the blues." Take care of yourself physically, exercise on a regular basis, get acquainted with your new surroundings, and become involved in your work. If you experience feelings of loss that seem to continue for longer than you would like or that interfere with your enjoyment of everyday activities, schedule a time with a counselor just for yourself through work, your church or a local mental health center. Within a short time you should be back on track and enjoying your new home, job and community.

For the great majority of families, the upheaval caused by a family move is usually a temporary one that dissipates with time and is balanced out by the excitement of exploring new surroundings, sharing new experiences, and making new friends. As you prepare for your family's journey to a new home, try to keep in mind that working together, sharing feelings, allocating responsibilities, taking care of yourselves emotionally and physically, maintaining a sense of humor as well as a sense of adventure and openness to whatever your new community might offer will allow all of you to enjoy, learn and grow from your moving experience.

Sources

1. Merrit, S. "Goodbye, House," *Parents Magazine*, May, 1990. 116-120.

2. Holmes, T. H. and Rahe, R. H.. "The Social Readjustment Rating Scale," *Journal of Psychosomatic Illness*, 1967, 213-218.

3. Kubler-Ross, E. *On Death and Dying*. New York: Macmillan, 1969.

4. Olkowski, T. and Parker, L. *Helping Children Cope with Moving*. York, PA: Gladden Publishing, 1992.

5. Ibid.

6. Ibid.

7. Janik, C. *Positive Moves*. New York: Weidenfeld and Nicolson, 1988.

8. The Piton Foundation. "Student Mobility: The Facts," *Another Generation*, Denver: The Piton Foundation, 1991, 3.

9. Buscaglia, L. *The Way of the Bull*. Thorofare, NJ: Charles B. Slack, 1973.

10. Herrick, T. "Transience Imperiling Pupils," *The Rocky Mountain News*, October 20, 1991, 93-94.

11. Kidson, P. *Iceland in a Nutshell*. Reykjavik, Iceland:Iceland Travel Books, 1974.

12. Copeland, L. and Griggs, L. "Culture Shock Is Part of Overseas Passage," *Overseas Assessment Inventory: Assessment and Development Guide*. Boulder: Moran, Stahl and Boyer, 1987

Note On The Moving Survey

In order to gather information and suggestions from our "kid experts" for children on the move, we devised a moving survey consisting of five questions to be used either as interview, classroom discussion, or written assignment topics.

The teachers who administered the survey proved to be tremendously creative in their presentation of the questions. They used them for classroom discussions, small group projects, interpersonal relationship activities, and homework and creative writing assignments. And they sent us their students' responses in lists, question-and-answer format, short essays, drawings, posters, "Dear Abby" letters, and even a tape of a class meeting.

We received ideas and advice from over 2,500 kids between the ages of 5 and 12 years of age from kindergarten to the 7th grade level in 19 different public and private schools representing urban, suburban, rural, and one island setting.

In administering the survey, many teachers discovered that not only is the topic of moving one that most kids can relate to but that simply discussing the survey questions helped students become more aware of the needs of new classmates as well as of those who might be facing a move in the near future. The questions also encouraged kids to share ideas with one another about adjusting to a new classroom or neighborhood setting, overcoming shyness, making friends, and working as a team. We hope their suggestions and advice work as well for you and your children.

If your child is entering or has just entered a new school or classroom because of either a family move or a change of schools, requesting that these or similar questions be addressed in his/her classroom may help make your child's settling-in process a more comfortable and enjoyable one.

Note On The Moving Survey

The Moving Survey Questions

1. Have you ever moved to a new school or a new neighborhood? If you have, what kinds of things did you think about and what kinds of feelings did you have? If you haven't, how do you think you would feel about it?

2. If you moved to a new school or a new neighborhood, what do you think your parents or your teachers could do to help you meet new people and make friends?

3. If you were new to a school or neighborhood and didn't know any other kids, what things do you think you could do to meet new people and make friends?

4. If you knew someone who was new to your school or to your neighborhood, what things do you think you could do to help that person meet new people and make friends?

5. If you knew someone in your classroom who was shy and had trouble making friends, what tips would you give him/her about how to meet kids and make friends?

An Invitation To Parents And Kids

We would like to hear from you and your children about your moving adventure. If your family has recently moved or is planning to move in the near future, we invite you to share your thoughts, feelings, concerns and experiences—both the triumphs and the disasters—with us.

We would like to know what strategies you and your children used to make your move an enjoyable one. If you used any of the ideas presented in this book, we would like to hear how they worked for you. And if your family came up with any ideas that you are willing to share, we'd love to hear about them.

Finally, if you have any specific questions that we haven't covered, please let us know. Send your comments and questions to:

> Denver Counseling and Psychotherapy Associates
> 1660 S. Albion
> Suite 900
> Denver, Colorado 80222

Additional information about workshops for educational, professional and community groups by the authors is also available through this same address.

Readings For Children

Non-fiction

Berry, J. *Every Kids' Guide to Making Friends.* Chicago: Children's Press, 1987.

_____ *Good Answers to Tough Questions about Change and Moving.* Chicago: Children's Press, 1990.

Beyton, C. *Berlitz Jr. French (Spanish) Dictionary,* New York: Aladdin Books, 1992.

Booher, D. D. *Help! We're Moving.* New York: J. Messner, 1983.

Conquest Corporation, *Teen Talk: Straight Talk About Moving...One Teen to Another* (Brochure/Poster). Birmingham, MI: Conquest Corporation, 1990.

Ervin, N. *Kids on the Move.* Birmingham, MI: Conquest Corporation, 1985.

Fassler, D. and Danforth, K. *Coming to America: The Kids Book about Immigration.* Burlington, VT: Waterfront Books, 1992.

Nida, P. and Heller, W. *The Teenager's Survival Guide to Moving.* New York: Antheneum, 1985.

Jarvis, J., McNaught, D., Reynolds, S. and Sibbitt, S. *Home Is Where My Heart Lives: A Workbook for Children on the Move.* Minneapolis: National Childhood Grief Institute, 1991.

Rogers, F. *Making Friends.* New York: Putnam, 1987.

_____ *Moving.* New York: Putnam. 1987.

Various Authors. *Gulliver Travels: A Kid's Guide to (Various Cities and States).* San Diego: Harcourt Brace, Jovanovich, 1988.

Fiction

Aliki. *We Are Best Friends.* New York: Greenwillow. 1982.

Asch, F. *Goodbye House.* Englewood Cliffs, NJ: Prentice Hall, 1986.

Balter, L. *Sue Lee's New Neighborhood: Adjusting to a New Home.* New York: Barron's, 1989.

_____ *Sue Lee Starts School: Adjusting to School.* New York: Barron's, 1991.

Berenstain, S. and Berenstain, J. *The Berenstain Bears' Moving Day.* New York: Random House. 1981.

Bresnick-Perry, R. *Leaving for America.* Emeryville, CA: Children's Book Press, 1992.

Clifford, E. *I Hate Your Guts, Ben Brooster.* Boston: Houghton Mifflin Company, 1989.

Conford, E. *Anything for a Friend.* New York: Bantam Books, 1979.

Dowling, P. *Meg and Jack Are Moving.* Boston: Houghton Mifflin Company, 1989.

____ *Meg and Jack's New Friends.* Boston: Houghton Mifflin Company, 1989.

Green, W. *The New House.* Batavia, IL: Lion Publishing, 1989.

Gretz, S. *Teddy Bear's Moving Day.* New York: Four Winds Press, 1981.

Hermes, P. *Kevin Corbett Eats Flies.* New York: Simon and Schuster, 1986.

____ *A Place for Jeremy.* San Diego: Harcourt Brace, Jovanovich. 1987.

Hughes, S. *Moving Molly.* Englewood Cliffs, NJ: Prentice Hall. 1979.

Johnson, A. *The Leaving Morning.* New York: Orchard/Jackson, 1992.

Jones, P. *I'm Not Moving.* Scarsdale, NY: Bradbury Press, 1980.

Korman, G. *The Twinkie Squad.* New York: Scholastic, 1992.

Leverich, K. *Best Enemies.* New York: Greenwillow, 1989.

Bao Lord, B. *In the Year of the Boar and Jackie Robinson.* New York: Harper and Row, 1984.

Lowry, L. *Anastasia Again.* Boston: Houghton Mifflin, 1981.

McKend, H. *Moving Gives Me a Stomach Ache.* Windsor, ONT: Black Moss Press, 1988.

McLerran. A. *I Want to Go Home.* New York: Tambourine, 1992.

O'Donnell, E. L. *Maggie Doesn't Want to Move.* New York: Four Winds Press, 1987.

O'Donnell, P. *Pinkie Leaves Home.* New York: Scholastic, 1992.

Park, B. *The Kid in the Red Jacket.* New York: Alfred A. Knopf, 1987.

Sharmat, M. W. *Gila Monsters Meet You at the Airport.* New York: Macmillan, 1986.

Siskin, L. *The Hopscotch Tree*. New York: Bantam Books, 1992.

Steele, D. *Martha's Best Friend*. New York: Delacorte Press, 1989.

____ *Martha's New School*. New York: Delacorte Press, 1989.

Szekeres, C. *Moving Day*. New York: Golden Book, 1989.

Tobias, T. *Moving Day*. New York: Alfred A. Knopf, 1976.

Waber, B. *Ira Says Goodbye*. Boston: Houghton Mifflin Company, 1988.

Watson, J. W., Switzer, R. E. and Herschberg, J. C. *Sometimes a Family Has to Move*. New York: Crown Publishers, 1989.

Winter, J. *Klara's New World*. New York: Alfred A. Knopf, 1992.

Winthrop, E. *The Best Friends Club*. New York: Lothrop, Lee and Shepard, 1989.

Wood, A. *Orlando's Little-While Friends*. New York: Child's Play, 1989.

Video Cassette

Tucker, K. and Murphy, J. *Let's Get a Move On!* Newton, MA: Kidvidz, 1990.

Audiotapes

Berlitz Jr. Italian (Spanish, French, German) for Children. New York: Aladdin Books, 1992.

Children's Living Spanish. New York: Crown, 1986.

Italian for Children. New York: McGraw Hill, 1988.

Lyric Language (French, German, Spanish). Carlsbad, CA: Penton Overseas, 1992.

Passport's Spanish (French, German, Italian) for Children. Lincolnwood. IL: NTC Publishing Group, 1993.

Readings For Parents

Books

Artenstein, J. *Moving: A Parent/Child Manual.* New York: Tom Doherty Associates, 1990.

Axtell, R. *Do's and Taboos Around the World.* New York: John Wiley and Sons, 1985.

Bainbridge, W. L. and Sundre, S. M. *School Match Guide to Public Schools.* New York: Arco, 1990.

Barrett, S. *Moving Right Along: The Complete Handbook to Survive Packing and Moving.* Los Angeles: Signals Publications, 1986.

Boyer, R. and Savageau, D. *Places Rated Almanac: Your Guide to Finding the Best Places to Live in America*, Englewood Cliffs, NJ: Prentice Hall, 1989.

Bunting and Lyon. *The Bunting and Lyon Blue Book: Private Independent Schools.* Wallingford, CT: Bunting and Lyon, 1989.

Burek, D. M., Koek, K. E. and Novallo, A. *The Encyclopedia of Associations.* Detroit: Gale Research. 1990.

Dickinson, J. *A Complete Guide to Family Relocation.* Lake Osweqo. OR: Wheatherstone Press, 1983.

Erickson, J. B. *The 1990-1991 Directory of American Youth Organizations.* Minneapolis: Free Spirit Publishing, 1989.

Georges, C. J. and Messina, J. A. *The Harvard Independent Insider's Guide to Prep Schools.* Boston: The Harvard Independent, 1987.

Gernand, R. *The College Board Guide to High Schools.* New York: College Entrance Examination Board, 1990.

Greenwold, D. *Coping with Moving.* New York: Rosen Group, 1987.

Harrison, C. *Public Schools USA: A Comparative Guide to School Districts.* Charlotte, VT: Williamson Publishing, 1988.

Hayes, N. D. *Move It! A Guide to Relocating Family, Pets and Plants.* New York: Dembner Books. 1989.

Janik, C. *Positive Moves.* New York: Weidenfeld and Nicolson, 1988.

Kohls. R. *Survival Kit for Overseas Living: For Americans Planning to Live and Work Abroad.* Maine: Intercultural Press, 1984.

Lechman, J. *After the Move*. Batavia, IL: Lion Publishing Corporation, 1990.

Martin, J. T. *The Livable Cities Almanac*. New York: Harper Perennial, 1992.

Muirhead, G. *Peterson's Guide to Independent Secondary Schools 1989-1990*. Princeton, NJ: Peterson's Guides, 1989.

Olkowski, T. and Parker, L. *Helping Children Cope with Moving*. York, PA: Gladden Publishing, 1992.

Piet-Pelon, N. and Hornby, B. *In Another Dimension: A Guide for Women Who Live Overseas*. Maine: Intercultural Press, 1985.

Roman, B. D. *Moving Minus Mishaps*. Bethlehem, PA: BR Anchor, 1991.

Rosenberg, L. and Rosenberg, S. *50 Fabulous Places to Raise Your Family*. Orange, CA: Career Press, 1992.

Sargent, J. K. *The Handbook of Private Schools*. Boston: Porter Sargent Publishers, 1989.

Schultz, S. *The Moving Handbook: A Time Saving Workbook to Help Organize Your Move*. Wilmette, IL: Abbreviations Press, 1989.

Thomas, G. S. *The Rating Guide to Life in America's Small Cities*. Buffalo, NY: Prometheus Books, 1990.

Ward, T. *Living Overseas: A Book of Preparations*. New York: The Free Press, 1984.

Resource Organizations For Families

Amateur Hockey Association of the United States
2997 Broadmoor Valley Road
Colorado Springs, CO 80906
719-576-4990

American Junior Golf Association
2415 Steeplechase Lane
Roswell, GA 30076
404-998-4653

American Montessori Society
150 Fifth Avenue Suite 203
New York, N.Y. 10011
212-294-3209

American Youth Soccer Association
5403 W. 138th Street
P.O. Box 5045
Hawthorne, CA 90251
213-643-6455

Association of Junior Leagues
660 First Avenue
New York, N.Y. 10016
212-683-1515

Boys Clubs of America
771 First Avenue
New York, N.Y. 10017
212-351-5900

Boys and Girls International Floor Hockey
P.O. Box 1653
Battle Creek, MI 49016
616-966-3432

Boy Scouts of America
1325 Walnut Hill Lane
P.O. Box 152079
Irving, TX 75015
214-580-2000

Resource Organizations For Families

Catholic Big Brothers
1011 First Avenue
New York, N.Y. 10022
212-371-1000

Camp Fire, Inc.
4601 Madison Avenue
Kansas City, MO 64112
816-756-1950

Council for Exceptional Children
1920 Association Drive
Reston, VA 22091
703-620-3660

Girls Clubs of America
30 E. 33rd Street
New York, N.Y. 10016
212-689-3700

Girl Scouts of the U.S.A.
830 Third Avenue and 51st Street
New York, N.Y. 10022
212-940-7500

International Soap Box Derby, Inc.
P.O. Box 7233
Akron, OH 44306
216-733-8723

Kiwanis International
3636 Woodview Trace
Indianapolis, IN 46268
317-875-8755

Lions Clubs International
300 22nd Street
Oak Brook, IL 60570
312-571-5466

Little League Baseball
P.O. Box 3485
Williamsport, PA 17701
717-326-1921

National Association of Hebrew School PTAs
160 Broadway
New York, N.Y. 10038
212-227-1000

Resource Organizations For Families

National Congress of Parents and Teachers
700 N. Rush Street
Chicago, IL 60611
312-787-0977

National Headstart Association
1309 King Street #200
Alexandria, VA 22314
703-739-0875

National Junior Tennis League
USTA Center for Educational and Recreational Tennis
729 Alexander Road
Princeton, N.J. 08540
609-452-2580

National Little Britches Rodeo Association
1045 W. Rio Grande
Colorado Springs, CO 80906
719-576-4990

National Lutheran Parent-Teacher League
123 W. Clinton Place Room 102
St. Louis, MO 63122
314-821-5135

Optimist International
4494 Lindell Boulevard
St. Louis, MO 63108
314-371-6000

Parent Cooperative Pre-schools International
P.O. Box 90410
Indianapolis, IN 46290
317-849-0992

Parents Without Partners
8807 Colesville Road
Silver Spring, MD 20910
301-588-9354

Pop Warner Football
1315 Walnut Street Suite 1632
Philadelphia, PA 19107
215-735-1450

Resource Organizations For Families

Rotary International
1560 Sherman Avenue
Evanston, IL 60201
312-866-3000

United Parent-Teacher Association of Jewish Schools
426 W. 58th Street
New York, N.Y. 10019
212-245-8200

United States Jaycees
P.O. Box 7
4 W. 21st Street
Tulsa, OK 74121
918-584-2481

U.S.A. Wrestling
225 S. Academy Boulevard
Colorado Springs, CO 80910
719-597-8333

United States Youth Soccer Association
1835 Union Avenue Suite 190
Memphis, TN 38104
901-278-7972

Young Men's Christian Association
101 N. Wacker Drive
Chicago, IL 60606
1-800-USA-YMCA

Young Women's Christian Association
726 Broadway
New York, N.Y. 10003
212-614-2700

Young America Bowling Alliance
5301 S. 76th Street
Greendale, WI 53129
414-421-4700

Acknowledgments

The original intent of the authors in compiling the data for this book was to gather and organize a list of practical suggestions that would be helpful to the millions of parents and children whose lives are affected by family moves each year. The authors wish to thank the thousands of children, parents and classroom teachers who shared their time and energy with us in response to The Moving Survey. We sincerely hope that this information will prove enjoyable and useful to families setting out on their own moving adventures.

We would like to give special thanks to those teaching staffs whose school-wide efforts in responding to our requests for aid made our task so much easier and enjoyable, in particular the following individuals and their faculty groups: David Livingston, principal, Polton Elementary School, Aurora, CO; Mike Volkl, principal, High Plains Elementary School, Englewood, CO; Dee Dee Martin, school psychologist, South Lakewood Elementary School, Lakewood, CO; James Brickey, principal, Cunningham Elementary School; and Barbara Wagner, headmistress, Graland Country Day School, Denver, CO .

We also wish to express our deepest appreciation to the following individuals, friends and colleagues for their contributions of time, energy, creativity and support: Charmen Olkowski, Aikahi Elementary School, Kailua, HI; Debby Larson Schukar and Andrea Lewis, Bromwell Elementary School, Denver, CO; Carol Carpenter, Prairie Middle School, Aurora, CO; Lita Phillips, Sally Stoker and Helen Simmons, Homestead Elementary School, and Elizabeth Barrett Kirk, Cherry Creek Campus Middle School, Englewood, CO.

And for those unique contributions that are the most difficult to classify but often the most wondrous to receive, we offer our thanks to Janice Steele and her sixth grade students at High Plains Elementary School, Englewood, CO for their delightful "Letters to Roger"; to Leo F. Buscaglia for being a wonderful friend and teacher; to Carol Waugh of Waugh and Rich Associates, San Anto-

Acknowledgments

nio, TX and Gay Hendricks for their forthright opinions of our earliest efforts and their invaluable suggestions for improvements; to Ruth Bleuzé and the youth training counselors at Moran, Stahl and Boyer, Inc. in Boulder, CO for sharing their experiences and insights about overseas relocations; to the staff of the Tattered Cover Bookstore in Denver, CO for their many suggestions regarding children's books related to moving; to Susie and Jake Phillips for letting us eavesdrop on a small portion of their lives; special thanks to Connie Platt for her enthusiastic support and editorial guidance; and loving thanks to Jeanne Hayes, president of Quality Education Data, Denver, CO, first, for her company's assistance in the compilation of the reading and resources list for parents and second, for taking time from a busy schedule to go computer shopping with her spouse when the trusty old Commodore finally gave up the ghost.

Finally, very special thanks to the young artists from Bromwell Elementary School in Denver, CO who shared with us their feelings about moving through their drawing: Sierra Boggess, Jennifer Brenneman, Alexis Grant, Robin Harris, Jennifer Judson, Regan Linton, Wynel Marchman, Rachel Nelson, Timothy Ridge, Mara Sobesky, Justin Thompson, Jessica Vigil and Ralonda Wafford.

Authors' Note

Portions of Chapter 9 of this manuscript have been previously published in article form under the titles "Family Move Can Be Shared Adventure for Everyone," *The Rocky Mountain News*, May 13, 1989, 1-H; "New Kids on the Block-Tips for Helping Children Adjust to a New Neighborhood," *Homebuyers of Colorado Magazine,* July/August, 1989, 41; and "Children Catch Attitudinal Drift from Parents in Move," *The Denver Post*, July 7, 1989, 5-G.

Portions of Chapter 6 have appeared in article form under the titles "Special Care Eases Trauma of Moving for Young Children," *The Denver Post*, March 11, 1990, 7-E; and "Psychologist Outlines Ways to Help Kids Cope with Moving," *The Rocky Mountain News*, March 11, 1990, 1-H.

Portions of Chapter 7 have appeared in article form under the title "Plan Ahead to Keep Kids Occupied on Moving Day," *The Rocky Mountain News*, November 16, 1991, 4-H.

Portions of Chapter 2 and 3 have previously been published by the authors in *Helping Children Cope with Moving*, Gladden Publishing, 1992.

The quote by Leo F. Buscaglia in Chapter 6 is used with the author's permission.

Index

dvice for kids from kids
  bout moving.............. 33
  ew friends 33-34
  ew neighborhood 34-35
  ew school................. 33-35
  achers 35
  orry 33
dvice for parents
  hild's feelings 38
  reating predicability 12
  iscussion tips.............. 36
  ostering involvement........ 13
  elping youngsters 12
  lf-awareness.............. 12

euzé, Ruth A. 147, 49, 158
ues, moving............... 163
scaglia, Leo.............. 61

aos-Survival Kit........... 56, 2, 83
ild's reaction
ve stages 22-23

D
Denial..................... 22
Disruption 24

E
Emotional disruption 18, 41
Emotional responses.......... 6
  preparation stage stressors 24
  settling-in stage stressors 26
  work stage stressors 25

F
Family dynamics............. 3-6
  gender roles 9
Fears of children............. 25
Feelings
  about new home 28
  around moving 11
  children 24
  confusion.................. 7
  expressing negative 46
  fears, children 61
  loss, children 61
  problems for kids 17
  teenager 7
  time for.................... 13
  younger child............... 7

Index

Foreign country, moving to.... 147
  cross cultural............... 148
  culture shock, four phases.... 156-157
  loss, sense of............... 153-154
  Message Moving Board...... 149
  new neighborhood.......... 156
  obtaining information........ 150-152
  pets, leaving................ 154
  Preparation stage............ 148
  questions, kids.............. 149
  special attention 153
  strategies 149, 152, 158
  travelling, preparation for 155
Friends, making
  discussion tips, parents....... 111
  don't push, parents.......... 134
  don'ts about, kids........... 123-125
  don'ts about, parents......... 125-127
  new neighborhood.......... 105
  new school................. 105
  preschool youngsters 134
  questions, kids.............. 105
  questions, parents........... 105
  school-age children.......... 135
  things parents can do 134
  tips for shy kids............. 109-111
  tips from kids 107-109, 115-119
  what kids want from parents .. 131, 133

G

Goodbyes
  children saying 61-62
  helping children say 62
  loss of pets................. 66
  parents 63
  special moves, death......... 64
  special moves, divorce 65
  symbols 63
Grab Bag Explorers 96

I

Isolation.................... 26

J

Job relocation 3

M

Mental health services 162
Message Moving Board....... 58
Moves
  unwanted 9
  voluntary 9
Moving
  don'ts about................ 123
  foreign country 147
  when to talk about........... 45
Moving day, strategies........ 74-76
Moving Journal.............. 53, 73
Moving principles
  assigned tasks 49
  fun and relaxation........... 50
  predictability............... 49
  proper equipment 50
  sense of involvement 49
Moving Survey 140
Moving tips
  parents 52
Moving tools
  family meetings............. 53
  Message Moving Board 53, 58
  organizing principles 49
  Premove Calendar........... 52
  Premove Checklist 52
  premove supplies, kids....... 50
Moving-in gift
  kids....................... 82
  parents 83

N

Neighborhood Discovery Board 92-93, 100
Neighborhood Map........... 94, 96, 101
Neighborhood Yellow Pages... 94-95
New neighborhood
  doubts and anxieties 89
  explore, how to 90-92
  exploring 89
  exploring, tools for 92
  exploring, Grab Bag 95
  exploring, parents 98-99
  exploring, telephone directory. 97
  first contact 162
  foreign country 156
  map....................... 81
  Neighborhood Discovery Board 82

Index

questions about 89
scrapbook 81
settling-in 25
settling-in stage 11
New school
  adjustments, first step 140
  different approaches, teachers . 140
  greatest concerns, kids 140
  Moving Survey 140
  stressful adjustments 139
  teachers, tips from kids 141
  teachers, tips from teachers ... 142

P

Packing 69
Parents' tasks
  acknowledging 89
  awareness 26, 89,
105, 132, 161
  encouragement 132
  information provider 29
  listening 106
  reassurance 28, 89,
106, 132
  role model 28
Patton Foundation 44
Post-move 22
Post-Move Calendar 81, 85
Post-Move Checklist 81, 83-84
Premove Calendar 52
  families 57
  parents 52
Premove Checklist
  kids 52-54
  parents 52, 55
Preparation stage 8, 21, 23
  cross cultural moves 148
  foreign country, moving to ... 148
  stressors on children 23
Problems for kids
  change 17-18
  confusion 17
  fears 25
  fear of unknown 21
  loss of privacy 21
  parental tension 20
  stressful experience 17

Q

Questions, kids
  about moving 37

R

Reasons for moves 8

S

Settling-in stage 11, 79
  length 161
  meaning 11
  resources 162
  stressors on children 25
Shy kids
  making friends, tips for 109
Stress
  disruption of routines 20
  keeping to a minimum 12
  reduction 50
  working stage 69
Stress in children
  signs of move-related 27
Stressors on children
  preparation stage 23
  settling-in stage 25
  work stage 24
Supplies
  moving-in, kids 80
  packing, kids 71-72
  premove, kids 50-51

T

Teamwork 6
Teenagers
  resistance 43
  strategies 18

U

Unpacking tips 82

W

When to move
  older youngsters 43
  potential difficulty 44
  preschool children 42
  school-aged children 42
  teenagers 43

Index

Work stage 10
  frustrations................. 69
  frustrations, reduction........ 70
  stressors on children......... 24
Worry...................... 26
  about parents 29
  younger child............... 7

Y

Yamamoto, Kaoru 17

Books by
GYLANTIC PUBLISHING

Teenage Addicts Can Recover: Treating The Addict, Not The Age
Shelly Marshall
Treatment providers & parents; 160 pages; $12.95; ISBN 1-880197-02-2, softcover
"Teenage treatment centers aren't working," says Ms. Marshall. The long term recovery rate for teenage addicts is less than 5%. Emphasizes the benefits of mainstreaming—improved recovery rates and cost savings for parents and society. Important pre-treatment issues are examined such as identifying the addict versus the abuser and choice of recovery programs. Covers aftercare, a necessary but slighted aspect of keeping the teen living drug free in today's environment. Illustrations–Bibliography–Index

AMEND Philosophy And Curriculum For Treating Batterers
Michael Lindsey, Robert W. McBride and Constance M. Platt
For treatment providers; 124 pages; $16.95; ISBN 1-880197-04-9, softcover
Abusive Men Exploring New Directions (AMEND). Philosophy and treatment necessary to work with perpetrators. Covers male gender training and battering, values-laden versus values-free therapy, characteristics of batterers, character disorders, aggression, the battering relationship, containment. Talks about procedures—the intake of court-ordered clients, therapeutic contract, first contact, obsessional thinking, crisis intervention, and the group process. Charts & Illustrations–Index

AMEND Workbook For Ending Violent Behavior
Michael Lindsey, Robert W. McBride and Constance M. Platt
For clients; 100 pages; $11.95; ISBN 1-880197-05-7, softcover
This is a tool for men in treatment for domestic violence. It addresses the perpetrator directly. The information and exercises challenge his ideas, allow him to think about how he lives his life, encourages discussion in therapy, and helps him develop skills to improve his life. Index

Set: ***AMEND Philosophy And Curriculum For Treating Batterers***
    AMEND Workbook For Ending Violent Behavior
For treatment providers and educators; $28.90, ISBN 1-880197-06-5, softcover

The String on a Roast Won't Catch Fire in the Oven: An A-Z Encyclopedia Of Common Sense For The Newly Independent Young Adult
Candice Kohl
Young adults; 194 pages; $12.95; ISBN 1-880197-07-3, softcover
The String... provides young adults with a source of practical information they might have missed—the unexpected expenses of renting an apartment; organizing a simple budget; maintaining a checking account; food shopping and storing basics; housekeeping; quality and cost; and ends with a potpourri of helpful hints. Resources–Index

Moving With Children: A Parent's Guide To Moving With Children
Thomas Olkowski, Ph.D. and Lynn Parker, LCSW
Parents; 196 pages; $12.95; ISBN 1-880197-08-1, softcover
Moving... helps parents understand and deal with the many feelings and behaviors of children when families move. Practical and effective suggestions to help families deal with the various stages of moving—from planning and discussing the move with their children to saying goodbye, packing and unpacking, exploring the new community, meeting new friends, and settling into the new home. Helps parents create a spirit of emotional support and teamwork with their children.

Helper: Bureaucracies Can't Help People, Only People Can
Sonja Jason　　　　Publication date: Late summer 1993
194 pages*　　　　$12.95　　　　ISBN 1-880197-09-X　　　softcover

Millions of people at some time have been, will be or are involved with two of societies most costly civilian bureaucracies, welfare and probation. There is no "average person" on welfare or probation because they come from every conceivable background. *Helper* is a series of vignettes about people and situations as seen through the eyes of the author who as a social worker and probation officer spent years working with people and the bureaucracies that were suppose to help them. The stories depict the wonder and diversity of human beings and the looniness of bureaucracies determined to fit people into rigid slots and deal with them accordingly. Sometimes the people are amusing, sometimes dangerous. *Helper* shows what doesn't work and what needs to change.

Dear Larissa: Sexuality Education for Girls Ages 10-17
Cynthia G. Akagi　　　　　　　Publication date: Late fall 1993
256 pages*　　　　$14.95　　　　ISBN 1-880197-10-3　　　softcover

A book for mothers (fathers) to give to their daughters. It is a mother's letters to her daughter about growing up—body changes, menstruation, boys, dating, love and sex—with space for personal comments. Many parents and their children are not comfortable discussing sexuality issues. *Dear Larissa* helps parents and daughters build communication in a caring manner. A book to be read and referred to by girls ages 10 through 17.

The Power of Touch: A Guide to Healing Sexual Abuse Through Poetry Therapy
Shelly Marshall and Kiley Kiebert　　Publication date: Late fall 1993
70 pages*　　　　$ 7.95　　　　ISBN 1-880197-11-1　　　softcover

The Power of Touch is a powerful self-help workbook of poetry therapy designed for victims of childhood sexual abuse. The book is organized in two sections—prose and poetry which is read first and a workbook which follows. The workbook is in three sections corresponding to body, mind/emotions and spirit. The theme is validation: This happened to me; this is how I think and feel about it; this is how I become whole again.

* Page count not firm at this printing
Prices valid in the United States only and subject to change without notice.

These bestsellers are available in your bookstore or order by calling, toll-free, 1-800-828-0113 to use your Visa/MasterCard.

Mail orders must include *complete payment* (check or Visa/MasterCard number with expiration date) unless you are a government agency, college, library or another official public organization, in which case please include a purchase order number.

Included $2.00 for shipping & handling with each order. Colorado residents need to also include 3.8% sales tax.

To ensure your order is properly handled, include the name and quantity of each title, your complete name and shipping address and complete payment. Thank you.

Send orders to:　　GYLANTIC PUBLISHING CO.　　　　(303) 797-6093
　　　　　　　　　P. O. Box 2792　　　　　　　　　　　FAX 727-4279
　　　　　　　　　Littleton, CO 80161-2792